MAKING THE
BUSINESS CASE

For my mother, Hannemor (1927–2008), whose love made everything possible.

Making the Business Case

Proposals that Succeed for Projects that Work

Ian Gambles

GOWER

Published by
Gower Publishing Limited
Wey Court East
Union Road
Farnham
Surrey GU9 7PT
England

Gower Publishing Company
Suite 420
101 Cherry Street
Burlington, VT 05401-4405
USA

British Library Cataloguing in Publication Data
Gambles, Ian
    Making the business case : proposals that succeed for
    projects that work
    1. Business planning 2. Project management 3. Proposal
    writing in business
    I. Title
    658.4'012

    ISBN: 978-0-566-08745-5

Library of Congress Cataloging-in-Publication Data
Gambles, Ian, 1962-
    Making the business case : proposals that succeed for projects that work / by Ian
Gambles.
       p. cm.
    ISBN: 978-0-566-08745-5
    1. Business planning. 2. Project management. 3. Proposal writing in business.
I. Title.
    HD30.28.G352 2008
    658.4'04--dc22

                                                                  2008033978

Mixed Sources
Product group from well-managed
forests and other controlled sources
www.fsc.org Cert no. SA-COC-1565
© 1996 Forest Stewardship Council

Printed and bound in Great Britain by
MPG Books Ltd, Bodmin, Cornwall.

Contents

List of Figures

List of Tables

Acknowledgements

Writing about how to make the business case has been a solo effort. Learning how to do it was just the opposite, and there would be pages and pages of acknowledgements if I were to recognise all those hard-working teachers, colleagues and clients from whom I have learned so much. I can mention only a few, whom I thank warmly for helping in different ways – Martin Chalmers, Virginia Grant, Simon Judge, Katherine Mathers, Andrew McDonald, Andrew Murray, Jonathan Norman, and Mike Stockdale. All the failings of the book are my responsibility alone. Finally I want to thank my father, Robert Gambles, for his support, and for writing wonderful books about interesting things.

① Introduction

'You will need a business case for that, of course.' These words, more and more common in both public and private sectors, can fill senior and middle managers with gloom and confusion. Why do we need a business case? Why can't we just do it? What exactly do they mean by a business case anyway? How am I going to get it done?

This is a hands-on guide to producing an outstanding business case. It is written for anyone, novice or expert, who needs to get a business case done, whether for a defined project or a broader programme, and wants to do it right. Before you can get stuck into the task, you need to understand the idea of the business case, why it is so prevalent, and how it is being used.

What is a Business Case?

This is less obvious than you might imagine. A business case is a recommendation to decision makers to take a particular course of action for the organisation, supported by an analysis of its benefits, costs and risks compared to the realistic alternatives, with an explanation of how it can best be implemented.

All too frequently, some of these critical elements are disregarded, which significantly undermines the value of producing a business case in the first place. Table 1.1 breaks the definition of a business case down into its component parts, explains why each is so important, and highlights what often goes wrong.

Table 1.1   A business case should be ...

Definition	Discussion	But too often...
A business case should be a recommendation ...	The recommendation gives the business case purpose and direction. The options may well be finely balanced, and decision makers may choose to take a different view, but without a recommendation the business case is simply a discussion paper.	It is not clear what is being recommended. Either the author wishes to avoid making a recommendation, or it is lost in a welter of data.
... to decision makers ...	A business case is designed to lead directly to a decision. So it must be aimed at those with the authority to make it.	Decision makers (sometimes through rules and processes of their own making) never see the business case, and the decision is made on the basis of a side paper.
... to take a particular course of action ...	The great strength of a business case lies in its specificity. You should be proposing a definite change, often to be executed through a project or a programme, and almost always requiring an investment decision.	The business case becomes a post hoc rationalisation for a decision already taken, or it degenerates into an over-long strategy document.
... for the organisation ...	Normally a business case is only worth writing for significant projects at the organisation or major business unit level.	Managers are asked to write a 'business case' for a laptop purchase or a staff party or some such. This is a waste of time.
... supported by an analysis of its benefits ...	The business case must say clearly why it makes the recommendation it does. This requires exegesis of the strategic rationale, as well as more detailed, systematic analysis of the specific benefits.	Benefits are either ignored, or presented in such an avalanche of jargon that the essential strategic purpose is buried without trace.

Table 1.1   *Concluded*

... costs ...	Cost estimation is often one of the most difficult aspects of writing the business case, but without it the case cannot be made.	Amazingly, some so-called business cases practically omit costs, citing lack of information. This is no excuse. Others present a mass of costing data but fail to analyse it meaningfully.
... and risks ...	Projects invariably involve risk, and understanding and taking ownership of risk is an essential part of the accountability which a business case invites decision makers to assume.	Risk is rarely ignored entirely, but proper focus on strategic risk can be lost if risk is relegated to an appendix preoccupied with secondary matters like risk management process or risk scoring methodology.
... compared to the realistic alternatives ...	If there really is no alternative, there is no decision to be made and no point writing a business case. Usually there is, and the best business cases are those which give decision makers genuine choices to make, making the recommended option stronger by testing it against reasonable, viable competitors.	Authors pretend there is no alternative, ignoring the fact that even an unavoidable external change (such as new legislation or the end of a lease) can meet a variety of credible responses from an organisation. Or unrealistic alternatives ('straw men') are presented to show the preferred option in a better light.
... with an explanation of how it can best be implemented.	Providing at least an outline implementation plan as part of the business case gives credibility to statements about timescale and dependencies which are often central to the argument.	Planning is consigned to a later stage in the process, after decisions have been taken, at cost to the realism and sustainability of the business case.

Why Have a Business Case?

Why put in the considerable time and effort necessary to produce a business case? There can be several reasons, and it is worth having a good grasp of the principal ones because it helps in understanding the value of the various component parts of a strong document.

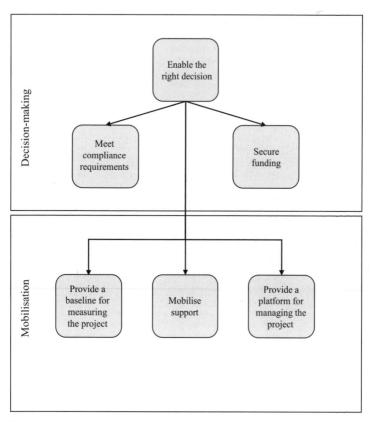

Figure 1.1 Purposes of the business case

ENABLE THE RIGHT DECISION

The single most important reason to produce a business case is to enable the right decision to be made. This may be something of a statement of the obvious, but a lot follows from it. All the components of the business case discussed in this book primarily serve this purpose. In particular, the need for a strong strategic rationale for the recommendation, and a robust comparative analysis of the costs, benefits, and risks of the options, flow directly from it.

Connected to enabling the right decision, as Figure 1.1 shows, are two more procedural, but nevertheless vital supporting roles which a business case must play in getting through to a decision point.

MEET COMPLIANCE REQUIREMENTS

The first supporting role is to meet compliance requirements, which will vary significantly from organisation to organisation. They may include:

● Requirements set by external grant-making or lending bodies – grant proposals are often business cases in all but name, and risk first-cut rejection if they fail to comply with rafts of tightly specified requirements affecting both the content and the presentation of the document.

● Requirements established through an overarching compliance regime. In central government in the UK, for example, projects and programmes are expected to go through the Office of Government Commerce's Gateway Review process at various stages in the project, and OGC reviewers will expect to see at least general compliance with the business case guidance set by HM Treasury.

● Requirements set internally through the wider corporate governance processes of the organisation, which can range from major corporate standards such as demonstrated achievement of specified Net Present Value targets through to conformity with centralised quality procedures all the way down to picayune points such as font size and colour selection.

Serious or trivial, right or wrong, these rules are put in place by organisations specifically to maintain standards and screen out at an early stage projects which fall short, so it is a legitimate purpose of your business case to demonstrate that your project is compliant with them.

SECURE FUNDING

The second supporting role is to secure funding. Fully compliant business cases which articulate a robust strategic rationale for the project they recommend can still be turned down, and regularly are, if they fail to convince decision makers to commit the necessary funds. Often a business case must succeed in a competitive environment, competing against other projects or calls on resources for access to investment. The true character and extent of this competition is sometimes only clear at the very highest levels, at the point where balance of investment and risk decisions are made. The consequence of this is that, in order to secure funds for the project, business case authors need to perform strongly not just in the nitty-gritty of getting the budget right and assembling a robust financial case, but also in the selling and stakeholder management activity which must accompany it. Stakeholder management and communications are covered throughout the book, and are the particular focus of Chapter 7.

A business case which fulfils these three linked purposes – enabling the right decision, meeting compliance requirements, and securing funding – will have got the management go-ahead for a project which is worth doing. So far, so good. But if it is sufficient only for these three purposes, there is a huge risk that the project will be stalled within a month; condemned to the fate of trickling small money out of the organisation without achieving any real results until someone takes a merciful axe to the whole thing. A good business case must also mobilise the project.

MOBILISE SUPPORT

Mobilisation means putting the project team in a position where it can move rapidly from winning a formal 'yes' to embedding broadly-based commitment to the project and demonstrating tangible progress. Breaking this down, there are three further purposes which a good business case should serve: mobilising support, providing a platform for managing the project, and providing a baseline for measuring the project.

Mobilising support is of course easier for some projects than others. There is always likely to be more support for building a new cancer ward than there is for an offshoring programme. In every case, however, there are likely to be key stakeholders to be won over, staff and other stakeholder communities to be reassured, sources of resistance to be managed, and project teams to be motivated.

Just as with the task of securing funding, the task of mobilising support is very unlikely to be achieved through the written word alone. It is the whole process of developing the business case which is the key to mobilising support, including identifying stakeholders, engaging with them to

7

understand their perspectives and interests, and constructing and communicating a solution which will deliver business benefits to stakeholders and meet their concerns. The role of the business case document itself is to articulate the rationale for the project in a succinct and compelling formulation which can be deployed by the sponsor and the project team to establish the ground on which any debate will take place.

PROVIDE A PLATFORM FOR MANAGING THE PROJECT

Mobilisation means mobilising to deliver as well as mobilising support, so providing a platform for managing the project is also an important role of the business case. The two elements which contribute most to this purpose are the implementation plan and the risk register.

The implementation plan, even if not particularly detailed, needs to set at least the early milestones and describe the main things which need to be done to get the project moving in the period immediately after approval of the business case. This will help to give the organisation and the project team a sense that the train has left the station and the journey is under way. It situates the project management activity correctly in the context of the delivery of the business case, and provides a preliminary basis for change control. It may also usefully incorporate proposals on the governance and management structure for the project, which may build on the governance and management structure for the business case and prompt decision makers to put these structures in place without delay and avoid leaving a vacuum in the wake of their decision. The risk register – if done right – embeds ownership of risks at a high level and kicks off the continuing risk management process.

PROVIDE A BASELINE FOR MEASURING THE PROJECT

If the business case has succeeded in:

- getting the right decision,

- meeting compliance requirements,

- securing funding,

- mobilising support for the project and,

- getting the project delivery moving,

it has accomplished a tremendous amount. The final role it needs to play is to provide a baseline for measuring the project. As the project moves forward, particularly in its early stages when it may still be politically vulnerable and may well run into teething troubles, it is bound to be challenged to justify itself afresh and demonstrate that it is really going to deliver. By setting out a schedule of deliverables, benefits and costs in the business case, the document becomes an authoritative reference point, both for the project team and for the wider organisation, and reduces the chances of the goalposts being moved.

Raising the Game

If a business case fulfils the definition set out in Table 1.1 and meets all the objectives set out in Figure 1.1, we can be pretty sure it is a good one. Plenty of business cases fall short, however.

Raising the game, preparing a business case which does all this, requires both competence and integrity.

Competence needs little discussion. We can all improve our competence and generally we all want to. You do not need to be technically expert in the subject matter of a project in order to write a business case for it, or trained in project management methodology or management accounting. The essential competence, aside from an aptitude for absorbing, interpreting and challenging expert advice, is knowing how to produce a business case. The purpose of this book is to help authors become more competent and proficient at preparing business cases.

Integrity needs some explanation. People tend to be deeply offended if you suggest they lack integrity. Lack of integrity, as we usually understand it, goes hand in hand with cheating, lying and generally two-faced behaviour at best, and at worst with fraud and betrayal. At least one staff appraisal process which I have experienced required managers to evaluate staff performance on a scale of 1 to 5 for a range of competencies, but offered only a Yes/No choice for the appraisal question 'Have they demonstrated integrity in their work?' I doubt if anyone dared to tick the 'no' box.

But we have to face facts. Many, many business cases submitted to decision makers show a conspicuous lack of integrity. Returns on investment are knowingly exaggerated in order to meet financial criteria. Project timescales are deliberately foreshortened, known sources of stakeholder resistance ignored or downplayed and significant technical difficulties

glossed over. Perfectly viable alternative options are suppressed altogether, or dismissed in a cursory manner, in order to allow the author's preferred option to stand tall among straw men.

This doesn't make the authors bad people. The working environment is full of political and career pressures which can make it difficult to be fully honest in a business case. And there is something both attractive and valuable in the passion and protectiveness managers can develop for their projects. But it does mean that the end product is a bad business case.

Integrity is a matter of degree. It is possible to be slightly less than wholehearted in making the argument for an alternative option, without actually omitting key points in its favour. There is a grey area, rather than a hard line, between being 'bullish' over timescales and being disingenuous.

TYPOLOGY OF BUSINESS CASES

If we look at competence and integrity as the two main variables, a simple typology of business cases emerges (Figure 1.2). Let us explore the four quadrants of this diagram in turn.

TOKEN BUSINESS CASES

Many business cases which lack both competence and integrity will be sent back for reworking. Weaknesses in argument and presentation make it easy for reviewers to spot weaknesses in evidence or attempts at manipulation and as a consequence either the project will be canned or the case sent back. So the bottom left group is often an unstable category, from which business cases will migrate into another quadrant. The principal exception to this is the *token* business case.

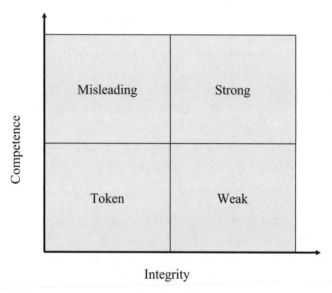

Figure 1.2   Typology of business cases

Token business cases are either for token projects or token decisions. Sometimes misguided organisation policies or weak management lead to situations in which a 'business case' has to be submitted for minor expenditure items such as laptop purchases, temporary staff appointments and so forth. (Some years ago I had to write a 'business case' for a mobile phone, a proposition which seems even more absurd now than it did at the time.) It is hardly surprising or culpable if the authors of these soi-disant business cases fail to take them very seriously. A more or less specious document is hurriedly put together ticking all the necessary compliance boxes without much regard for substantive argument, because none is really merited. Usually the decision maker will not even read the document and will automatically give approval unless they have a budgetary crisis or a personal distrust of the author. This is all quite pointless activity, and it would be better management for the issue to be briefly discussed and decided without paperwork, with approvals documented in an email if necessary.

On other occasions, the issue may not be a token one but the business case becomes token because the decision itself does not really exist. This often applies to so-called 'business case updates'. In the middle of a multi-year change programme, for example, producing a fully revised business case can be a time-consuming and expensive undertaking, as the programme will inevitably have moved some distance from the original business case. Yet unless the future of the programme has been called into question, there is no decision to be made, and the exercise is a distraction, adding little or no value to the suite of programme reporting which should be part of the normal course of business. The requirement may even be perceived as a threat, potentially destabilising delicate stakeholder consensus or re-opening debate on first principles at a time when forward momentum is critical to success. A fractured and inconsequential document is the likely result, deliberately skirting the major issues of the moment and positively inviting senior management not to read it.

WEAK BUSINESS CASES

Turning to the lower right quadrant of Figure 1.2, weak business cases are those put together with honest intent to enable decision makers to make the right decision about a project and give it a strong foundation, but which fail to do so because they are simply not well done. Typical areas of weakness include:

- vague or excessively high-level or generalised propositions;

- non-sequiturs or long passages of irrelevance in the strategic rationale;

- narrowness of vision; preoccupation with tangential issues;

- impenetrability of language; reliance on poorly understood technical or business jargon; preoccupation with methodology at the expense of substance;

- incompleteness, particularly in the project plan, costings or risk register;

- arithmetical or modelling errors in the costings;

- vaguely defined benefits, or failure to quantify any benefits;

- ambiguity in the governance arrangements;

- failure to reflect adequately the interests of key stakeholders, or to carry out stakeholder management and communications activity early enough.

The consequences of a weak business case can be serious. Least serious – except perhaps for authors – is if the weakness is spotted by reviewers or decision makers and the case is remitted for rework. Even this can lead to delay and to loss of reputation.

Should a decision be taken on the basis of a weak business case, it will inevitably have a random character. Without clarity of argument, relevant, accurate information, or effective stakeholder management, decision makers will have to fall back on prejudices, hunches and horse-trading. The eventual decision will be whatever pops out of that lottery machine.

Even if by luck or good intuitive judgement a sound decision is taken despite a weak business case, this is not the end of the story. Weakness in the business case is like a chronic disease in the project, leading to problems such as breakdown of management control, inability to monitor progress or expenditure, failure to manage resistance, project collapse, or, worst of all, completion of the project without delivery of benefits.

MISLEADING BUSINESS CASES

Turning to the top left quadrant of Figure 1.2, the nature of a misleading business case brings us back to the vexed question of integrity. Misleading cases are professionally executed, thorough and carefully structured and argued. But they use these qualities to draw decision makers either towards the wrong decision entirely, or into the right decision but without sufficient awareness of the challenges and risks involved. There is practically no limit to the variety of forms the misleading case can take. Some are very calculated and manipulative, some spring from delusion and wishful thinking, while others are semi-conscious or even subconscious, leaving truth and rigour behind in a turn of phrase, a selective reading of a vital piece of evidence, or an undue deference to the known or perceived preferences of the decision makers. A well-known case study – even if not exactly a business case – is highlighted in Figure 1.3. The problems in this very public example are replicated with significant business consequences in numerous business cases which ultimately fall on the misleading side of the line.

Some of the more prevalent symptoms of the misleading business case are:

- Forecasts – particularly revenue forecasts but also cost estimates, efficiency savings, audience figures, or any other relevant volumetric – adjusted to be just sufficient to meet Net Present Value or other known corporate targets.

- Delivery timescales foreshortened, by unreasonably aggressive assumptions about the duration of activities on

Much of the protracted and bitter debate about the US and allied attack on Iraq in 2003 has revolved around the presentation of evidence that Iraq had covert holdings of weapons of mass destruction. The key statements of the allied case in this area were General Powell's presentation to the United Nations Security Council on 5 February 2003 and the UK Government's dossier of 24 September 2002. Both were flawed, as has been admitted in retrospect, and each provides a different illustration of the many ways in which a case can become misleading.

Lord Butler's *Review of Intelligence on Weapons of Mass Destruction* (HC 898, The Stationery Office, 14 July 2004) is a masterly study into how, without anyone involved in the production of the UK dossier setting out to mislead, the omission of caveats, the influence of suspicion of Iraq on the selection of evidence, and the preference for eyecatching claims created a cumulative impression which in the end turned out to be false.

The US presentation to the UN, which was more explicitly designed to make a case against Iraq, was affected by these and worse problems, including reliance on intelligence from a source already known as a liar, and has been branded 'dead wrong' by a presidential commission (Commission on the Intelligence Capabilities of the United States Regarding Weapons of Mass Destruction, 31 March 2005). 'The main problem,' according to one senior former US foreign service officer, 'was that the senior administration officials have what I call faith-based intelligence. They knew what they wanted the intelligence to show.' (GregThielmann, quoted in CBS 60 Minutes, 4 February 2004).

Figure 1.3   WMD in Iraq

the critical path or the realistic possibilities for workstreams to progress in parallel. These assumptions may not be documented or may not be given adequate prominence.

- Nelson's eyeglass syndrome – turning a blind eye 'accidentally on purpose' to significant sources of stakeholder resistance or hard-to-mitigate risks.

- Spin, especially in the case for change. The obligatory 'do nothing' option is sometimes little short of a caricature, declaring serviceable but ageing equipment 'obsolete' or focusing exclusively on the limitations of a current organisational structure and disregarding its strengths.

- Straw man options. These are depressingly common, and can range from heavy-handed and extreme options which simply take up space in the business case to more subtly unacceptable options which mask the potential for realistic alternatives.

The damage done by the misleading business case can be far-reaching and usually cannot be rectified by competent project management. Not only will decision makers have selected the wrong course of action, they will also have bought into an articulate line of argument behind it and communicated their commitment to it to stakeholders and staff. The opportunity cost of the mistake can never be recovered and often the momentum the ill-founded project acquires leads to good money being poured after bad in a downward spiral ending only in post-project recriminations.

STRONG BUSINESS CASES

The challenge is to locate your business case firmly within the upper right quadrant of Figure 1.2, delivering a strong business case which is thoroughly and skilfully put together and lacks nothing in integrity.

Figure 1.4 illustrates this typology with an example of how the same issue can be presented to very different standards of competence and integrity, to very different effect.

The rest of this book is a guide to how to produce a strong business case. Each chapter covers a different element of the work and follows a similar format. A golden rule addressing one of the most critical points in that area heads the chapter. The principles involved are then explained, accompanied by

Misleading	Strong
'Financial targets cannot be met without a redundancy programme. The programme proposed in the preferred option is expected to affect as few as 100 mainly more junior staff and pays back in less than five years. Industrial relations issues are fully covered in the programme's risk mitigation strategy.'	'Option A will lead to between 100 and 150 redundancies, mainly at Grade 4, saving c. £2.5m p.a. but incurring termination costs of £10m. An impact assessment of each affected site is at Annex J; there is a significant risk of industrial action at Croydon where some 20 per cent of the job losses will occur.'
Token	**Weak**
'The change programme has inevitably led to some redundancy costs, fully funded in this year's budget. Savings will start to accrue from next year. Details are in the spreadsheets at Annexes D, E and F.'	'Option A is likely to lead to some redundancies, yielding long-term paybill savings at the cost of significant investment. It has not yet been possible to quantify these impacts. Affected staff wil not welcome the change and there may be some industrial relations issues.'

Figure 1.4   Typology illustrated

some analysis of issues and techniques illustrated by one or more examples. Each chapter concludes with a brief recap of the contents and an exercise, designed to help you quickly absorb the learning from the chapter; recommended answers are at the back of the book.

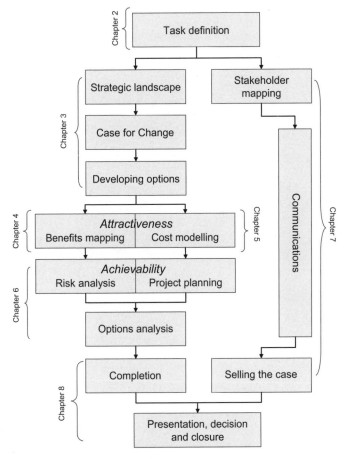

Figure 1.5   Flow of activities

The flow of the guide broadly follows the flow of activities which you will need to carry out in order to produce an effective business case, illustrated in Figure 1.5 (see previous page), although, as will become clear, many of these activities are interdependent, making iteration unavoidable. Some activities run largely in parallel, or at least can do if resources are plentiful and time is scarce.

2 **Task Definition**

Golden Rule

*Well begun is half done. Make sure you are tackling the right task,
with appropriate resources and structures, before you start.*

It may be a distant and painful memory, but most of us have had
to sit exams at some time in our life, and the feeling of having
just been asked to produce a business case can be not unlike the
feeling of sitting in front of a blank piece of paper with a pen, a
clock and an exam question. Except worse. Because more often
than not, it is not clear what the question is.

There is, typically, an assortment of information along the
following lines:

- a commissioning email explaining the importance of the
  project and noting that it 'needs a business case';

- a verbal briefing from a senior manager, emphasising how
  pleased they are that you are up for the job and how much
  they are relying on you;

- a date for a board meeting of some kind to consider the
  business case, often much too soon; and

- a miscellaneous collection of documents about the project,
  full of optimism and empty of numbers.

If you are better off than this you are in a good starting position with few grounds for complaint. The key message here is that *identifying and clarifying the question is a fundamental part of the responsibility of the business case author.* No-one will lay the question out for you. You have to figure it out yourself.

There can be no formula, of course, for identifying the question. Careful reading and analysis, and persistent and direct inquiry are the only tools available. Challenge is essential, as the question set out in your brief, if you have one, may often not be the right question, and you will need to drill down further. This is the time to ask 'why?' before the process acquires a momentum of its own and the organisation expects the business case team to answer that question itself.

Pinning down the real question requires addressing both substance and process.

Issues of Substance

There are three linked parts to the issue of substance: the *nature of the project*, the *derivation and status of the budget* and the *context of prior decisions*.

NATURE OF THE PROJECT

What is the nature of the project or programme for which the business case has been commissioned? It is important to be comprehensive in this enquiry, even if the answer appears obvious. For example, if the business case is about building a new corporate headquarters, it is essential to establish whether the question is as open as 'how should we meet the apparent requirement for increased central capacity?' or as closed as 'which construction company should we select to build our chosen design on our chosen site?'

The business cases these different questions would require are quite different, from a straightforward procurement project at one end of the spectrum to a complex business design, requirements forecasting, estates planning and build/buy sourcing programme at the other. On no account start work trying to answer the closed question until you are confident that the open question is no longer on the table, or you could be completely wasting your time. Thorough investigation is essential in all cases to avoid a false start. This applies across the board, to all kinds of projects and programmes, but look out particularly for business change projects masquerading as technology projects; this occurs regularly because it is so much easier to latch on to IT performance weaknesses than to recognise whole system failings.

DERIVATION AND STATUS OF THE BUDGET

Managing the financial elements of the business case is often the hardest part of the work, as so many areas of potential difficulty, including cost estimation, commercial confidentiality and propriety, accounting treatment, sensitivity analysis, and so on are brought into play. I will have more to say about this later (see Chapter 5). At the task definition stage, the prerequisite is to understand the derivation and status of the budget.

Derivation means what the budget has been or will be primarily based on. The two alternatives are bottom-up – the budget is based primarily on a detailed costing of the project activities and deliverables needed to meet the requirement – and top-down – the budget is based primarily on a high-level allocation of funds reflecting senior management's prioritisation of the project in the context of available resources and competing demands on them. Status means whether the budget is fixed or variable. Are decision-makers expecting to review and change the budget, or would that be regarded as a project failure? This gives us four main types of budgetary situation, shown in Figure 2.1.

Knowing the derivation and status of the budget will enable you to define the task, particularly the task of completing the

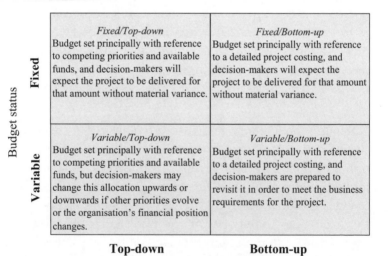

Figure 2.1   Status-derivation of the project budget

economic appraisal, within the most appropriate paradigm. While in every case the objective is to identify and specify options which provide the greatest benefit for the lowest cost, this is merely axiomatic and does not actually help guide the emphasis of your investigation. Consider the chart of paradigms shown in Figure 2.2.

Challenging   If the budget is fixed on the basis of a top-down allocation, the key question to answer is how, and indeed whether, the project can deliver the benefits the business wants for the available funds. In some cases it may be that it cannot, and you must be alive to this possibility from the outset and ready to push back both on the aspirations of the project team and sponsors, and/or on the resource limits set by management. This may mean challenging senior individuals at early stages in the process, which is itself a challenge, but

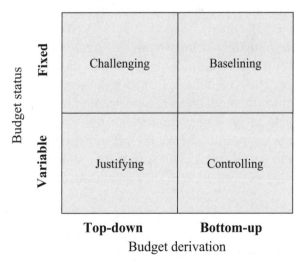

Figure 2.2   Project budget – chart of paradigms

the price of not doing so may be emerging from the task definition phase with an unachievable task. In that event the business case can, and should, state clearly that the project is unachievable within the available budget.

Baselining If the budget is fixed on the basis of bottom-up costing, the scope for major changes is likely to be limited. The business case author's focus therefore needs to be on validating and documenting the financial baseline for the project. Have any significant errors or omissions been made? Is the approach already the most cost-effective? Has adequate contingency funding been allowed? In this situation, expectations are likely to crystallise quite early into targets and they must be validated before it is too late.

Justifying If the budget is set as part of a top-down process but is liable to change, whether upwards or downwards, the task you face is to justify the allocation – or indeed to seek to amend it – by thoroughly costing the project and demonstrating the implementation consequences of the likely range of allocation decisions. These conditions heighten the temptation of being drawn into the production of a misleading business case (see Chapter 1) and it is important to balance a reasonable desire to protect the position of the project in the pecking order for funds with the imperative of showing – and ultimately being able to deliver – value for money for the allocation.

Controlling If the budget is derived from a bottom-up costing process but has not been effectively fixed or capped, the project sponsor and project manager may be in clover, but the business case author has a potentially tricky task. The business case must assess the level of investment that the likely benefits for the organisation actually justify, and thus in these circumstances act as a control mechanism on the scope and scale of the project as well as on the inevitable tendency to introduce financial padding and over-generous overheads.

CONTEXT OF PRIOR DECISIONS

Understanding the nature of the project, and the derivation and status of the budget, needs to be complemented by obtaining full information about relevant prior decisions. It is very rare for a business case process to be initiated with a blank slate, with all options open and no givens. There is nothing wrong or surprising about this, for development of core business strategies and creative brainstorming exercises should precede the more significant investment in preparing a business case on a specific issue. Business cases and blue skies do not mix well.

Unfortunately, it is also rare for the context of prior decisions to be crystal clear, internally consistent, and properly documented. Again, however, this is not surprising, as the need to clarify choices, write down arguments and reconcile competing stakeholder interests is one aspect of the typical need for a business case, and it falls to the business case author to sort it out at the earliest possible stage in order to define the task ahead.

If *all* the significant decisions have already been taken, there is a risk that what is required is a token business case (see Chapter 1). Producing these is a thankless and largely purposeless task to be avoided if at all possible. In most cases, however, it pays to dig a little deeper and use the task definition phase of the business case activity to expose cracks and ambiguities in the decision structure which the business case itself will later repair and resolve. It is important at this stage:

- to get and keep a copy of all documented decisions;

- to use initial discussions with the project sponsor, project team and key stakeholders to understand their perceptions of the context of prior decisions; and

- to begin to form a view as to which of these real or perceived decisions are authoritative and which can and should be re-opened or put under pressure in the interests of widening the field of play for the business case.

The case study shown in Figure 2.3, which is closely based on an actual case, illustrates how important it is to get to the bottom of all three of the issues of substance: the nature of the project, the derivation and status of the budget, and the context of prior decisions.

Issues of Process

Defining the task is a matter of process as well as substance. If you are not clear about the process, you run a real risk of having a brilliant business case in your head, which you cannot get produced, read, or acted on. The three key processes which must be addressed are:

1. document rules and conventions;

2. timescales and resources;

3. governance.

DOCUMENT RULES AND CONVENTIONS

The business case should never be seen primarily as a document. Refer back to the definition provided on page 1 – a business case is an analytically supported recommendation. It would be unusual, but not out of the question, for the business case to be a series of structured presentations to key decision makers, supported by some key numbers and lot of dialogue and debate.

The Department of Public Delivery had an ageing IT infrastructure and decided to invest in a major desktop modernisation project. A strong business case was prepared and a supplier selected. At the same time, the department was at an earlier stage of work on a number of smaller projects to modernise inward and outward facing applications such as its records system, intranet and web presence. Management decided to bring all these projects together into a single programme, appointed a programme director and requested a business case for the programme. A robust approach to task definition was essential to preparing the ground for the right sort of document.

Asking open and probing questions about the nature of the programme revealed that while much of the implementation work and most of the cost related to IT delivery, the essence of the programme was strategic. The programme was needed to enable the organisation to design and enforce a common direction for multiple projects in order to realise an ambitious information strategy which was otherwise at risk of being largely aspirational. The business case authors therefore needed to define a clear direction for the programme.

Examination of the derivation and status of the budget suggested an essentially variable/bottom-up budget, qualified by some concern from decision makers about the risks of overall programme cost increases. A core part of the business case task was to improve the programme level understanding, control and executive authority over project budgets, seeking to build a programme contingency fund and to integrate tighter financial management processes into the governance and management arrangements.

Exploring the context of prior decisions exposed – perhaps not surprisingly – a tendency for project managers to make tendentious claims that their projects had been 'approved', their budgets 'ringfenced' and their suppliers 'selected'. Closer scrutiny revealed that while the main infrastructure replacement contract had been awarded, the majority of other commitments were no more than provisional, and the eventual business case successfully argued for a number of projects to be put on ice for two years to allow for a managed pace of change.

Figure 2.3   Case study – task definition

Certainly a document on its own will hardly ever suffice, and supporting activity is discussed further in Chapter 7.

Usually, however, the document is an important part of the case, and it is essential to know what document control rules (explicit) and conventions (tacit) are in place in the decision-making organisation.

Such rules and conventions can apply to structure, presentation or length. They may be derived from published authorities or they may be local standards set by a corporate standards team or inherited from an influential previous document or author. Presentation may be required to follow corporate branding and quality standards, occasionally specified at a surprisingly detailed level to include font sizes, graphic presentation standards and so forth. It may also be heavily but informally influenced by the known preferences of the chief decision maker. Length can be a potentially sensitive subject, prone to bizarre edicts, usually emanating from secretariats, such as 'all Board papers must be no more than three pages'.

In all these cases, pragmatism and a sense of proportion are priceless assets. Having defined the substance of the task, the true supporting role of the document becomes clearer, and hence the extent to which it is important to pay scrupulous attention to these various rules and conventions. For example, if the main decisions have already been taken and the purpose of the business case document is to elaborate the baseline for the project, make it as long and detailed as it needs to be and structure it for ease of use by the project owner, project management and the project team, then give the board a two-page executive summary – because it really does not matter if they read the full business case or not. Again, if the true decision maker is external to the organisation (such as a funding body), then concern yourself with researching *their* standards, and ignore the fretting of the in-house quality team.

TIMESCALES AND RESOURCES

The cost-time-quality trade-off is by now a commonplace and certainly applies to the production of business cases. What is important about this trade-off is not merely being aware that it exists; it is too obvious to be interesting that a top-quality document is going to require more time and resources than a quick and dirty one. The important point is to understand from the outset which of the variables are under your control and to what degree, and to manage inputs and expectations accordingly.

Control over production deadlines is a luxury rarely available to the business case author since the business case is typically inserted into the project development process at a relatively mature stage – or driven by an external deadline – rather than itself initiating or leading it. There is little point in railing against this situation, which is after all only logical from a wider business perspective. Far better to take advantage of imposed timescales to highlight to decision makers the implications of the cost-time-quality trade-off, making the entirely reasonable point that inadequate resources in inadequate time will produce inadequate quality as inevitably as night follows day, so that if time is fixed then there needs to be some flexibility on resourcing.

31

You need to establish what the human resources available to you as business case author are. How big a team you need of course depends on the scale and complexity of the project and the type of business case required, but for most projects you are likely to need individuals to whom you can confidently assign responsibility for:

- collecting, challenging and estimating numbers;

- financial modelling;

- understanding business strategy;

- stakeholder management and communications;

- preparing drafts and reports;

- project planning;

- project tracking and progress chasing;

- facilitating workshops;

- assessing benefits and risks.

An immediate and often vexed question is whether this multi-skilled set of human resources can all be identified in-house, and released to a sufficient extent from their current duties to contribute to the business case at the necessary level. For substantial business cases, this is rarely possible, and it is a massive mistake to seek to make do with poor quality human resource from the bench or well-intentioned promises of support from individuals who are in reality fully committed elsewhere. This may leave no choice but to look for contract support.

Contracting for support in developing a business case can be approached either by contracting for inputs or contracting for outputs. Contracting for inputs means recruiting and integrating individual specialists into the business case team to provide services to the team leader – the business case author. Contracting for outputs means selecting a consultancy company to deliver the business case to the sponsor, leaving it to them to construct the appropriate team. Both approaches are valid, and the choice must depend on circumstances. Table 2.1 highlights the advantages and disadvantages of each and the sort of indicators to look for in making your choice.

Either way, hiring consultants is of course a significant investment in the business case process, which may have the incidental advantage of focusing the commissioners' mind. It is difficult to justify laying out cash on a non-value-adding exercise such as the production of a token business case, so such endeavours may fall by the wayside once significant resources are demanded.

GOVERNANCE STRUCTURE

The question of contracting for support can also sometimes highlight the need for clarity in the critical area of governance. Few things are more likely to be fatal to a project than a misconceived governance structure, and the production of the business case is not immune.

Table 2.1   Contracting for business case professional services

	Contracting for inputs	Contracting for outputs
Advantages	Greater client control Easier to change course/make adjustments midstream Option to use known individual experts Easier to integrate with in-house team More opportunity for you or your own staff to learn new skills from the contractors Easier to remove poorly performing contractors Better commercial rates	Easier to run a meaningful competition Opportunity to benefit from experienced suppliers' innovative approaches and benchmarks Greater cost control possible through firm price contract Disciplined, focused team Branded supplier can be held accountable for deliverables
Disadvantages	Time absorbed in complex team management Unproductive tensions among competing contractors Too many accountabilities Time and materials contracts offer no incentive for timely completion	Overall cost likely to be higher External team may be remote from real business and stakeholder concerns Places considerable management demand on sponsor Few obvious performance measures, so you may just have to take what you are given Some suppliers may be preoccupied with selling on their own role in project delivery, thus losing objectivity
Best choice when ...	There is a strong business case author and a strong core in-house team with some gaps in expertise There are significant uncertainties over core business strategy Trusted contractors with unique knowledge of the business have already been identified (in this case it may be possible to draw these individuals on to the client side, and contract out a discrete work package to a bigger organisation on output terms)	The project is very large and technically complex The case for some action is clear and the budget for the business case work is known There is a realistic prospect of transferring some financial risk at the business case stage

The business case phase has specific governance requirements. Figure 2.4 illustrates an ideal governance structure for the business case work. The model is deliberately simple, as over-elaborate governance structures are usually unworkable. In large organisations or partnership projects there may need to

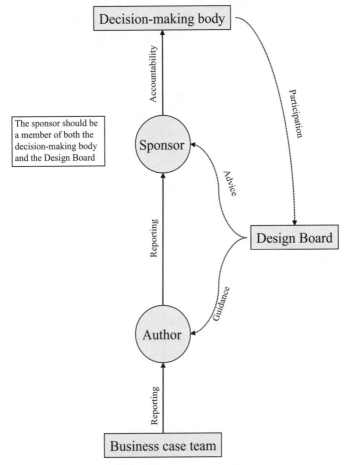

Figure 2.4   Governance

be more complex variants, but it is important to retain an underlying clarity of structure.

The component parts of the model are:

- *The Decision-making Body.* This could be the main board of the organisation or a less senior group, depending on the nature of the decision. In certain circumstances it could be an individual (a wealthy donor, for example). The critical criterion for a good governance structure is that it is clear who is empowered to make the final decision on the business case. Ambiguity can creep in surprisingly easily in this area and must be determinedly rooted out. For example, what happens if the budget rises above a certain financial threshold? What happens if the business case identifies a need for operational, or HR, or environmental changes, and the relevant interests are not represented on the purported decision-making body? What does the decision-making body need to do to re-establish its authority?

- *The Sponsor.* The sponsor of the business case is the senior individual who is driving the business case. She or he is accountable to the decision-making body and will normally be a member of the decision-making body. If not, there are likely to be significant difficulties from their lack of positional authority and a second, über-sponsor, will probably have to be identified. The sponsor needs to have a genuine commitment to the success of the business case, preferably combined with a measure of objectivity about the possible options. They also need the clout to mobilise resources and to shift obstacles which the author cannot, and enough time available to devote to senior stakeholder management.

- *The Author.* The author not only writes the business case document, but should also take responsibility for the whole process of delivering a successful case, including planning and directing stakeholder management and communications activity, and managing the business case team.

- *The Design Board (or Advisory Board).* The exact structure of advisory and consultative arrangements put in place around the business case process will depend on the situation. In a few cases it may be possible to dispense with them altogether and rely on proactive stakeholder management and communications to avoid the danger of the business case team working in a silo and losing touch with the requirements of the business. Normally, however, there are advantages to corralling the more influential of the internal stakeholders into a structured advisory body, here labelled a design board as its purpose is to provide advice to the sponsor, and guidance to the author, on issues which must be addressed in the design of the business case options. The desired relationship between the design board and the sponsor is that of a critical friend. It may well be appropriate for some members of the decision-making body – those with the greatest stake in the outcome – to be engaged in the process through the Design Board and thus bought into the conclusions of the business case while it is being produced.

It is worth noting and guarding against some of the more common problems with governance. Table 2.2 lists three red issues, which are near-certain causes of failure, and three amber issues, which will pose a serious risk to success and should be avoided if possible.

Table 2.2   Potential governance problems

Issue		Comment
Red	**No remit/ accountability**	The decision-making body must be expecting the business case, ready to make a decision, and holding someone accountable for presenting it to them. Without this the governance structure has a broken neck.
	No sponsor	If a remit comes directly to an individual or team at the working level, or is directly contracted out, the gap where the sponsor should be will kill the business case, unless it was a token exercise all along. The sponsor is essential to enabling the decision.
	Committee authorship	While many people will be involved in producing the business case, and there is plenty of opportunity for utilising innovative collaborative tools and techniques to engage participation across the business, a business case without a controlling mind is adrift, and cannot achieve the rational cogency needed to take the project forward.
Amber	**Chief Executive as sponsor**	There may sometimes be no-one else to sponsor the business case apart from the CEO, but the inevitable elision between the decision maker and the sponsor is fraught with risk. The role of external critical friends and, where possible, peer review assumes much greater significance in preventing the business case degenerating into a personal manifesto.
	Sponsor and author the same	Again, in small organisations there may sometimes be no alternative, but for the sponsor to be drawn into the heavy time commitment involved in actually producing the business case is likely to pose both practical problems of time management and more serious challenges of personalisation. It is always a warning sign when people begin consistently to talk about 'Bob's business case' rather than 'the X project business case'.
	Committee sponsorship	While not as definitively fatal as committee authorship, committee sponsorship is best avoided too. It is good to have many voices raised in support of the business case, but different players inevitably and properly have different interests and roles, and the author is likely to end up coping with conflicting messages and priorities, while the key messages conveyed at decision-making level are diluted through compromise. A single individual sponsor is much better placed to broker a way forward.

Conclusion

This chapter has explained the importance of defining the task carefully at the outset of work on the business case. Do not accept your brief at face value. Probe what the question really is, and why it is being asked one way rather than another. Focus in particular on the following points:

- *The nature of the project.* What is the project really about? Should you be producing a business case, for example, to identify the best way to build five new prisons, or the best way to align supply and demand for prison places? Make sure you are not producing a business case that answers the wrong question.

- *The derivation and status of the budget.* Has the budget already been fixed or not? Is it based on a detailed bottom-up costing or a central allocation? This makes a big difference to the role of your business case in budgeting and financial control for the project.

- *The context of prior decisions.* How much has already been decided? What are those decisions and how solid are they? These are often shifting sands, and it is important to find out what you must take as a given and where you need to challenge and clarify.

It is also important to get the process right, and the following process issues were covered in this chapter.

- *Document rules and conventions.* Find out the ones which you must follow to achieve compliance where compliance matters, and stick to them.

- *Timescales and resources.* Usually there is little flexibility over deadlines, so you are likely to deliver a poor quality output unless you get the right resources from the outset. There is a wide range of skills you must be able to draw on, and often this will require external support. Choose carefully between integrating specialist contractors into your own team or contracting out the whole task.

- *Governance structure.* A dysfunctional governance structure can kill a business case, and you need to ensure that your own role as the author is correctly positioned with respect to the decision-making, sponsorship, and advisory roles.

Defining the task carefully will get the business case off to a good start before a single word is written.

Chapter 2 Exercise: Young Brothers

Young Brothers have manufactured specialist dolls in Leicester for 60 years. Five years ago they closed most of their UK workshop and contracted out production and packaging to a partner in China. Design and quality assurance are still handled in Leicester. You are a locally based independent consultant and Mr Young has asked you on the phone if you could write a business case for the expansion of the business through a major investment in internet marketing and direct distribution. He will pay all reasonable fees and give you all the internal resources and access you need. He is available for a 30-minute briefing tomorrow before you begin and has asked you to email in advance five or six questions you want to ask him. What are your questions?

③ From Strategy to Options

Golden Rule

Know the case for change backwards. If you understand the strategic space you are working in, and what you are really trying to achieve, structured creative thinking will produce winning options.

This chapter takes us to the heart of the decision around which all business cases should revolve. What is the organisation going to do? What decision should be made, what action taken? Having invested the necessary time and effort in defining the task (Chapter 2), we are now ready to move on to finding the right answer. Turn back to the flow diagram (Figure 1.5 on page 19). This chapter covers the three crucial stages of understanding the strategic landscape, building the case for change and developing options.

Understanding the Strategic Landscape

DISTINGUISHING BETWEEN THE BUSINESS CASE AND THE BUSINESS STRATEGY

The relationship between a business case and a business strategy is a complex and important one. For example, purchasing a large-scale customer relationship management system for the first time will be driven by the business's marketing strategy, but is also likely to drive future changes in it. This relationship is sometimes referred to as 'strategic fit' and it can be a difficult relationship to grasp, but understanding it is vital to the success of the business case.

The first principle to follow is that the business case should not be a strategy. There may be fuzzy parts of the boundary and crossover between one and the other, but they must be kept as distinct as possible. A strategy exists to set direction, providing a reference point which different parts of the organisation will use to guide their planning and activity. While a good strategy will certainly contain specific commitments to action, it must also be cast in sufficiently high-level terms that it remains robust through changing conditions at least for the medium term. A business case, in contrast, is always associated with a particular decision and drives one course of action, and usually leads to a defined and time-limited project. Mixing them up is bad for both. A strategy approached as a business case will tend to lack vision, radicalism and ambition, and may quickly become irrelevant as its overly specific cost-benefit analysis is overtaken by events. A business case approached as a strategy will tend to become woolly and unfit for purpose, and may also arouse opposition if it is seen to be seeking to exercise influence in areas outside the proper scope of the project.

The second principle to follow is that the strategy must come first and that the sponsor and author of the business case need to know what it is. This seems blindingly obvious in theory, but it is not necessarily so in practice. Changes in core business strategy can have a dramatic impact on the validity of the objectives of the business case, and the tendency for strategy development to be carried out in relatively tight groups creates a real risk of a business case being built on a set of assumptions about strategy which fall apart by the time the case is presented for decision.

MAPPING THE STRATEGIC LANDSCAPE

This brings us to the imperative of understanding and mapping the strategic landscape. It is rarely only one strategy that needs to be considered. More often, there will be a whole environment of strategies which the business case author will need to identify, understand and map in order to locate the business case correctly. Which strategies and how many will, of course, depend on the nature of the business and the business case. The key indicators which the Board uses to track the performance of the business may offer a good starting point for exploring the strategic landscape. Increasingly, both public and private sector organisations are making use of a balanced scorecard or equivalent tool to encourage an appropriately multidimensional approach to business management, and the scorecard will itself have been developed by taking a broad view of business strategy and priorities.

For example, if an oil company asked you to produce a business case for the redevelopment of a flagship company-owned petrol station, it would be fraught with danger to proceed to options identification and cost-benefit analysis equipped only with an understanding of financial strategy expressed in targets for revenue, turnover and return on capital. This might lead to an apparently highly cost-effective set of options which fell foul of, among others:

- The brand strategy – what kind of image are the company's front-line premises expected to present in the next few years?

- The environmental strategy – does the company expect to go beyond meeting statutory standards and invest in leading edge environmentally friendly facilities or promotion of alternative fuels?

- The estates strategy – does the company wish to continue owning its own forecourts?

Similarly, a business case for a new training centre for a local authority would need to consider at least:

- The training strategy – what sort of training is actually going to have to be delivered and in what way?

- The estates strategy – what is the wider strategy for developing authority owned or leased premises versus use of external facilities?

- The diversity strategy – how will the authority's statutory duties to promote diversity affect its approach to training?

- The HR strategy – how big is the in-house workforce going to be in future?

- The IT strategy – what kind of platform will training need to run on within the new facility, now and in three years' time?

Mapping out this strategic landscape can be done partly on the basis of an understanding of the organisation, its business and how the Board is approaching it, but it will also require investigation and testing through stakeholder interviews. A glance at the examples should suggest that there is a clear link here between the process of laying the right intellectual foundations for the business case – ensuring that all relevant factors have been understood – and laying the foundations for stakeholder acceptance. Interviewing the IT director about the new training centre business case will not only ensure that you are aware of the difficult issues around the interface between the training system and the live system, but also make it much less likely that she will throw this problem into the mix at the eleventh hour to spike your case because you have failed to consult her. Asking open questions at this stage enables the business case author to construct a full view of the strategic landscape at the same time as beginning to build support and manage expectations.

How this understanding of the strategic landscape is recorded and connected to the options development process is to some extent a matter of personal style. There is much to be said for a visual representation, sketching out in diagrammatic form the array of strategies which create the strategic space within which the business case must succeed. Others find mind-mapping approaches and software tools helpful. It is in any event important to avoid making this a purely reductive stage. The journey from strategy to options is the principal creative moment in the business case enterprise and opportunities may be overlooked if there is too much of a rush to narrow down the field of vision.

Building the Case for Change

Having gained a thorough understanding of the strategic landscape, the next step, and an essential precursor to options development, is to construct the case for change.

WHY HAVE A CASE FOR CHANGE?

The case for change serves three purposes:

1. It steers the options development process by identifying and beginning to explore the most important reasons for taking action, thus providing an initial set of evidence on which creative thinking can be grounded and a tangible basis for evaluating options.

2. It gives the business case team, including of course the sponsor, some solid early material to build momentum for action among key stakeholders, beginning to tackle organisational inertia and resistance to change well before the preferred option is known and camps have begun to form for and against it.

3. It pre-empts the notorious problem of 'Option 0', the 'do-nothing option'. Option 0 is sometimes actually a requirement of the business case process, yet its value is itself usually zero and sometimes less. Why bother producing a business case if the best option is not to make any changes? A strong case for change deals up front with the (perfectly reasonable) question 'can't we just leave well alone?'

DRIVERS

The heart of a good case for change is an analysis of drivers. What are the factors which are driving or will drive change? It is a good idea to make a list, and as with all such lists an even better idea to keep it simple. There are only five things we need to know about each driver:

1. *What is it?* Summarise in as few words as possible what it is which is driving the need for change.

2. *What sort of driver is it?* Use a simple typology to help you organise your thoughts; this could be either the range of strategies mapped across the strategic landscape, if they are suitable, or a standard categorisation tool such as PESTLE (Political, Economic, Sociocultural, Technological, Legal and Environmental).

3. *How powerful is it?* Ideally, express the weight of the driver in measurable terms. If that is impossible, give an honest, plain language assessment to help sort the genuinely business critical drivers for the project from the nice-to-have free riders.

4. *Who owns it?* For stakeholder management, it is important to know whose expectations the business case is going to have to satisfy, or justify disappointing.

5. *Where's the evidence?* The business case team needs to document on what source it is relying for the assertion that a particular driver exists and is relevant to the business case options.

An example tabulation of drivers, picking up on the petrol station redevelopment example discussed earlier, is shown in Table 3.1.

THE IMPORTANCE OF EVIDENCE

The last column of this table is vital. The case for change stage of business case preparation is not about imaginative problem solving. It is about evidence gathering. One of the reasons why it is so important to ensure at the task definition stage

Table 3.1 Cataloguing drivers for change: an example

Driver	Description	Category	Strength	Ownership	Evidence
Sales	Need to achieve regional sales growth targets	Financial	Critical – regional target likely to be 20 per cent undershot without redevelopment at flagship sites	Regional Sales Director	Monthly sales trend analysis. Competitor Analysis Team benchmark data
Partnership	Need to provide appropriate facilities at this site for supermarket partner	Marketing	Critical – failure to redevelop prime locations will undermine or even breach partnership contract	Senior Marketing Director	Partnering contract. Marketing Director interview record
Brand	Need to improve and upgrade site to support branding strategy	Marketing	Secondary as ROI not clear; but must find some way of addressing current negative site image	Brand Support Team Leader	Site customer survey data. CEO feedback
Safety	Need to upgrade underground fuel storage	Environmental	Tank renewal needed within 3 years to maintain corporate safety standards	Regional Distribution Manager	Engineer's report

that you have access to appropriate human resources to do the work of business case preparation, and that the timescales for completion of the business case are realistic, is that a strong business case must be evidence based. Referring back to our typology of business cases (Figure 1.2), evidence bolsters the competence of the final product, and, provided it is not utilised or presented too selectively, its integrity as well.

The impact of a small number of well-supported and relevant data points in the case for change, marshalled inside the strategic space where the business case needs to operate, can be huge. Although obtaining and interpreting it is often fraught with difficulty, benchmark data is particularly valuable in this respect. Qualitative evidence is also important, even if it consists only in the *obiter dicta* of a Board member or key customer; there are significant benefits both for stakeholder management and for the audit trail in being able to quote authoritative sources in support of non-quantifiable arguments for change.

Obtaining good quality evidence, particularly if the business case lies in a complex strategic landscape, takes time and effort. Securing the resources to do some real research, even if it has to be rapid and highly targeted, will pay dividends.

CONSTRAINTS

As well as cataloguing and analysing the drivers for change, it is also important to do the same for the constraints on change. Constraints are not the same as risks, which will be discussed at greater length in Chapter 6. Risks are factors which may or may not adversely affect the progress or success of the implementation of the preferred option and risk management activity should be designed to minimise their impact. Constraints are factors which limit the range of viable options which can be put forward in the business case. The purpose of focusing on constraints in the case for change is not, at this stage, to try to find a way of accommodating them, but to identify – and carefully scrutinise – the boundaries for developing options to respond to the drivers.

Constraints can be catalogued in the same tabular format and under the same headings as drivers. There is, however, a particular aspect of the assessment of the strength of each identified constraint which merits further attention. There is a real danger of allowing the options development process, and therefore the whole business case, to become hedged in by exaggerated or imaginary constraints. Typically, in the business case team's fact-finding interviews, they will come up against assertions that a proposed course of action 'could not be done' or 'would be against the rules', or that some feature of the existing system or process 'has to be retained' because of the law or the unbending requirements of the customer or of corporate procedures. Sometimes this is true, and it would be catastrophic to ignore the constraint in the development of options. But sometimes it just isn't. Law and regulation often become conflated with custom and practice, and the way something has always been done comes to seem the only way it could possibly be done and hence, with just a short flight of fancy, the way it must be done. Always, always insist on seeing the regulation itself and make sure you understand it. Then ask what it would take to change it. It is particularly important to distinguish between the established expectations of the (internal or external) customer and evidence of their real needs, between statutes and rules and, in the special case of government business cases, between primary and secondary legislation. Challenge and scrutinise all constraints before accepting and documenting them.

An illustration of a table of constraints, using the petrol station redevelopment example, is shown in Table 3.2.

A thorough analysis of drivers and constraints provides all the necessary raw material for a sound, evidence-based case for change. While obviously this is too soon to be starting to write up the business case itself, it is not too early to write a first draft of the case for change. Kept succinct, and hammering home the business critical drivers with hard facts, a short statement of the case for change can be a very powerful tool for building support for the business case, flushing out drivers and constraints not yet recognised before it is too late and framing the debate on options. It is also a good discipline for the business case author and the team, serving to re-focus activity and prevent the team from losing the plot amidst the inevitable accumulation of paperwork and points of view.

Identifying Options

The journey from strategy to options was characterised above as the principal creative moment in the business case enterprise. All business cases are about change and if there is a road less travelled out there that leads to a better way forward for the organisation, this is the time to find it. Options identification

Table 3.2   Cataloguing constraints: an example

Constraint	Description	Category	Strength	Ownership	Evidence
Return on Investment	Preferred option must achieve corporate target of 15 per cent return on investment	Financial	Critical – business case will not be considered if this test is not met	Finance Director	Corporate Business Strategy FD interview record
Ownership	Lease on site expires in four years Options must pay back in three years and/or include costed appraisal of opportunity for renewal	Estates	Critical – options will be ruled out if this constraint is not reflected in the analysis	Estates Manager	Site lease
Green credentials	All publicly visible investment must earn a 'green tag' by being realistically presented as contributing to corporate environmental performance	Environmental	Very important – approvals board will refer back for further work if credible green options are not included	Marketing Director; Green Team Leader	Corporate Business Strategy document. Green Team bulletin
Access	Need to ensure forecourt and shop redevelopment options meet or exceed statutory requirements for access for the disabled	Compliance	Secondary as access is not a problem on the present site – but must ensure this is not overlooked	Statutory Compliance Team	Disability Discrimination Act 1995. Compliance Team guidance

is not the same as options analysis, which comes later in the process, and it is a mistake to exclude interesting possibilities too early just because there are seemingly intractable challenges to resolve.

Options identification is best handled as a three-step sub-process. Whatever labels are applied to each step, and however they are managed in procedural terms, remember the sequence 'close-open-close'. The field of options must be narrowed, opened out and then narrowed again. Figure 3.1 illustrates this, and we will then discuss each of the three steps in turn.

The first stage of options identification is *framing*. This means setting the framework within which options need to

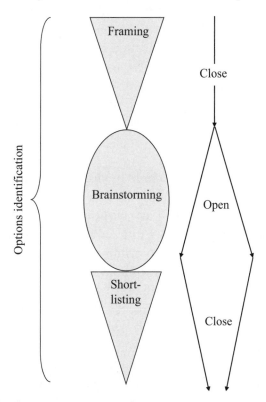

Figure 3.1   Options identification

be identified. The good news is that you have already done this and it is simply a matter of restating the work in order to give some shape to the creative forces you are about to unleash. This is the time to refer back to the task definition work already carried out (see Chapter 2) and the presentation you have developed of the case for change. Remember that identifying and clarifying the question is a fundamental part of the responsibility of the business case author. The groundwork put in with the project sponsor and other key stakeholders now enables you to articulate with confidence and authority what the question is. Write it down, and use it to frame the options identification process. The reason this is a 'close' phase of the process is that you simply cannot afford to divert creative energy or resources into considering options, however brilliant, which do not answer the question put, because they will not enable you to execute the task you have been assigned.

This sets the stage for the 'open' *brainstorming* phase. In this phase it is the combination of structure and creativity which will deliver results. As well as providing the framework for the brainstorming process within which options are to be identified, you also need to stimulate and direct creative energies by structuring the brainstorming itself. A useful technique is to explore different possible answers to the basic questions about the project – what, where, who, and how?

● *What?* Within the agreed framework, are there different options for what the project is going to deliver? Is it a lowest-cost standard design petrol station or could it be configured as a one-stop auto centre fully integrated with the supermarket partner? Is there a market for full service?

- *Where?* Is location one of the constraints or are there options? Thinking back to the example of a new local authority training centre, does it have to be on an existing site? What about a hub and spoke model?

- *Who?* Who is going to deliver the project or the service? Should outsourcing be considered? Are there potential partners?

- *How?* How should the objectives be achieved? In a change programme, for example, are there alternative 'big bang' and incremental approaches? In an IT project, are there possible choices between a dedicated infrastructure and a web-based approach?

This structure will encourage creative thinking as well as focus it. There are many good techniques and resources for stimulating creative thinking in a brainstorming exercise. Familiar but important wisdom is that brainstorming should not be an evaluative process – original thinking will often be self-censored if individuals, particularly those in less senior positions, feel vulnerable to criticism or scorn if they volunteer an off-the-wall idea which clearly will not meet the key criteria for success as it stands but may contain the germ of an exceptional solution. An externally facilitated off-site workshop with the core team at this stage is often a modest investment with a huge return. The team by now will understand the issues better than anyone, and may need to be away from the preconceptions of senior stakeholders in order to release their thinking from narrow channels.

In addition to facilitating group conversations about possible options, it can also be productive to try to generate ideas by stimulating people's visual and lateral thinking capabilities. Inviting people to sketch a picture of the project, of a pair of 'before and after' pictures, draws out different aspects of the creative mind and stimulates laughter and enthusiasm, which always help. An experienced independent strategic advisor can also play a valuable role in stimulating ideas, perhaps using proprietary tools such as Edward De Bono's *Six Thinking Hats*.

The third and final stage of options identification is *shortlisting*. A good brainstorming exercise will produce a large number of candidate options, many more than it is realistic to evaluate properly within the business case. They need to be winnowed. It is important *not* to do this by giving the sponsor a red pen and inviting him to strike them out. This is both arbitrary and demoralising. Run an exercise to assess the benefits and concerns associated with each candidate option in the light of the task definition, the strategic landscape, the drivers, and the constraints. The quality of the list of benefits will give an indication as to whether the option has enough to offer (relative to the other candidates) to make it worth pursuing. The seriousness of the concerns will give an indication of whether it is worth doing some preliminary investigation to see whether they can be allayed.

Conclusion

This chapter has explained how to develop options for consideration in the business case. There are three steps:

1. *Understanding the strategic landscape* is essential to ensuring that the business case options are consistent with the wider business strategy. There are usually several different strategies to take into account, and finding out what they are and mapping the strategic landscape will pay dividends both in terms of the relevance of options and their acceptability to stakeholders.

2. *Building the case for change* deals with the perfectly reasonable prior question 'should we do anything at all?' This is mainly about gathering and analysing evidence – identifying, challenging, and documenting the drivers for the project and the constraints on the selection of options. Preparing a strong, succinct case for change helps to ground options identification and is also a powerful communications tool.

3. *Identifying options* is the key creative step, taking the framework set out in the strategic landscape and the case for change and using brainstorming techniques and the creative energies of your team to generate a range of different options for delivering the project objectives, from which you can then draw up the shortlist to take forward.

Taken together, this suite of activity will enable the team to progress to the next stage of business case preparation

(Chapters 4–6) and to step up its campaign of advocacy with stakeholders (Chapter 7), from a strong, creative foundation.

Chapter 3 Exercise: Irish wind farms

The Republic of Ireland has no natural fossil fuel reserves, and oil and gas prices are rising. The Government faces a combination of pressures to provide for the needs of a rising and increasingly urbanised population and a growing light industrial capacity whilst meeting domestic political demands to meet or exceed international carbon emissions targets. As a major part of its response to this challenge, the Government is considering supporting a series of large-scale wind turbine farms on the west coast. Reaction from local communities to initial consultation on the scheme has been mixed, with opposition from traditional farmers, tourist enterprises and second-home owners, but support from the local working-age population. Energy companies are playing a waiting game at the moment. You have been tasked with preparing the overarching programme business case for the Taoiseach's office. You have worked with your sponsor to define the task, and established that there is a clear political commitment to going ahead in some form, but an open mind about scale and modalities. Affordability is also a big issue.

Using this information and your general knowledge, spend a few minutes on each of the following:

a) List the strategies you will need to obtain and understand in order to map the strategic landscape for the business case.

b) Draw up a table of the top three drivers for the project, using the template in Table 3.1 on page 50.

c) Exercise your mind – suggest a couple of options which might be worth exploring.

(4) Benefits

Options Analysis

By this stage you should have an evidence base, an understanding of the strategic landscape, a case for change, and a shortlist – or at least a not unmanageably long list – of options. The next step is the big one, analysing the options to identify and make the case for the recommended course of action. It is common knowledge that this involves looking at the benefits, costs and risks of each option and comparing them. Actually getting this done is usually a demanding and difficult job, and there are many traps for the unwary. The next three chapters aim to guide you through the task of options analysis.

Before launching into consideration of benefits, costs, risks and plans, it is worth standing back for a moment to recall why you are looking at them in the first place. This will help provide some sort of protection against the temptations of taking either a dangerously cavalier or suffocatingly detailed approach to the task. Turn back to Figure 1.1 on page 4.

The first reason is to enable decision makers to make the right decision. This means that it is essential for all the factors relevant to the decision to be assessed honestly and stated clearly. If your method is too complicated or your reasoning abstruse, you will never be able to present it persuasively, and decision makers will go back to their prejudices and intuition.

The second reason is to support the mobilisation of the project by providing an authoritative reference point – a statement of benefits, a cost estimate, a draft risk register, a preliminary implementation plan – which sets the project on a sound footing and provides a baseline against which subsequent progress and change can be measured. This means that the task has to be approached with thoroughness and rigour. Playing clever games with costings or finessing risks at this stage is storing up big trouble for later, and does neither the project nor the organisation any favours.

ATTRACTIVENESS VS. ACHIEVABILITY

A strong, simple tool which often appeals to decision makers is the attractiveness-achievability chart (Figure 4.1). This is as easy as it looks. Options are placed on the chart by measuring their attractiveness on the y axis and their achievability on the x axis to give each option a unique set of co-ordinates. Broadly speaking, options at the top right are good – options which offer plenty of benefit at reasonable cost and can probably be delivered. Bottom left is bad – options which offer limited benefit and/or incur excessive costs, and also present a significant risk of failure. I will say more in Chapter 6 about how you can use this chart to help you identify and make the case for a preferred option.

For the present, consider the attractiveness-achievability chart as an objective. How can it be completed in any meaningful

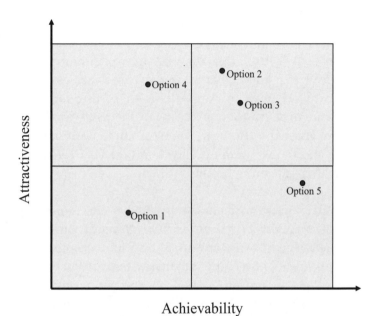

Figure 4.1   Attractiveness-Achievability chart

way, how can you assess the attractiveness or achievability of the options on the shortlist? Assessing attractiveness is a matter of comparing benefits against costs. Assessing achievability is usually a matter of looking at the combination of deliverability and risk. Let's start with attractiveness and, within that, let's begin with benefits.

Benefits

There is a substantial body of literature about benefits mapping and benefits realisation, and a plethora of consultants ready to help you with them. In many ways this is a good thing.

Prior to the spotlight being turned on benefits in this way, there was a lurking tendency to shrug off systematic analysis of benefits as just too difficult, and not worth much in any case since we all knew what we were trying to achieve, didn't we? Analysis tended to concentrate on costing alternative approaches to delivering a project whose necessity was already taken for granted, with the inevitable result that vast amounts of time and money were expended on projects which in the end yielded little or no business benefit.

To populate the attractiveness-achievability chart for options assessment, *quantifying benefits must be attempted*. Quantifying cost is relatively straightforward, at least in conceptual terms (but see below for how easy it is to make a hash of it in practice), because there are proven methods for comparing any form of cost – be it incurred at different times, in different currencies, with different degrees of certainty, and so on. Quantifying benefit is much harder, because in many cases the benefits of a particular proposed project are not just financial. As well as income or savings from a project, there may also be, to name just a few, improved staff morale, reputational benefits, better quality of service to customers, environmental benefits, wider economic and social benefits, and a greater likelihood of achieving the non-financial strategic goals of the organisation. How to get started with all this?

STEP 1 – FOCUS ON PROJECT OUTCOMES

Different options will offer different levels of benefit of course – otherwise there would be no need for an analysis. But it is a big mistake to set off to try to assess the benefits of different options without first establishing the benefits of the project.

This gives you the currency of comparison. Why is the project being considered? What are the positive outcomes which decision makers want? The benefits of the project should be embedded within the case for change, and that is the place to start identifying them. If you have already prepared a good list of drivers, that list should correlate closely with the list of benefits of the project. Try to keep the list of benefits short, as otherwise both the diagrams and the calculations to follow become exponentially more complex and less persuasive. Pay attention also to the language in which benefits are articulated. Whereas outputs (see below) must be sharply defined, observable and measurable, benefits may or may not have those characteristics, but they must come across as ends not means, outcomes not outputs.

To illustrate this point, and the development of the benefits map and the weighting and scoring process, we will use throughout this chapter the hypothetical project to build wind farms in Ireland set as the Chapter 3 Exercise. A simple illustrative table of drivers for this example is in Table 9.1 on page 169. Reflecting on the goals of this project, we would probably identify no more than five important benefits: energy security, compliance with international obligations, a better environment, economic development in the West of Ireland, and public support for the alternative energy strategy.

STEP 2 – EXCLUDE MONEY BENEFITS

It is of course a benefit of a project if it saves money or produces more revenue. But such positive cashflows should not be treated as a benefit for these purposes, because they can be more accurately factored into the financial analysis. If one of the options in our example is expected to save 50 million euro each year through reduced oil imports, that figure should obviously feature as an annual saving on the costing spreadsheet (see Chapter 5). If savings from lower oil imports are also shown and scored as a benefit, that is double counting.

You will also need to exclude any non-cash benefits which you have decided to convert into cash figures and factor into the financial analysis. For example, there are methodologies for attaching monetary values not just to operating efficiencies which cannot actually be converted to cash, but also to benefits and disbenefits as diverse as traffic jams, fresh air and death. There are different views about the 'monetisation' of benefits, and corporate policies may make it difficult to follow the approach recommended here, which is to avoid it. There are in some cases interesting philosophical aspects to this, which are addressed in Figure 4.2, but even if you set no store by those considerations, or take a different view, there are still serious practical problems with monetisation.

The first of these is that it obfuscates the costing. Handling costs in the business case is, as explored in the next section, fraught with difficulty, and the whole area is rich in scope for catastrophic error. Relatively few people are really confident tunnelling into the construction and assumptions of complex financial estimates, and the job of the business case author is to make cost accessible, not sacrifice the clarity of the figures by introducing various kinds of 'funny money'. The second is that, unless monetisation is taken to ridiculous extremes, there will almost always be some benefits which have to be factored in by another route such as weighting and scoring

According to Her Majesty's Treasury's 'Green Book', which provides more or less prescriptive guidance to UK government departments on project appraisal, 'the valuation of non-market impacts … should be attempted wherever feasible'. The Green Book cites approvingly work by the Department for Transport which 'attributes monetary values to the prevention of non-fatal casualties, based on a Willingness to Pay approach. Serious and slight casualties are valued separately and the values are uprated in line with changes in GDP per head. Values currently in use for preventing a serious and slight road injury are £128,650 and £9,920 respectively (at 2000 prices)'.

It is terribly easy to mock this sort of thinking, but the troubling reality is that it dominates much decision making by both public and private institutions. This utilitarian approach is rooted in the late eighteenth century ideas of Jeremy Bentham, who first articulated the principle of utility, the rational calculus of maximising pleasure and minimising pain for the greatest number of individuals, as the only valid foundation for morality, law and public policy (*Principles of Morals and Legislation*, 1781). Yet Bentham's target was really action based on subjective, religious, or arbitrary principles, and his utilitarianism in the raw has long been left behind in the development of political philosophy, which has for generations now emphasised human rights and various interpretations of the social contract as the foundations for ethics and public policy. The failure of narrowly utilitarian thinkers to value common goods in general and the environment in particular led to much highly destructive decision making over more than a century and the development of new techniques for monetising environmental impact is a belated attempt to deal with the fact that most people, and therefore most of the stakeholders in any project, do not exercise their judgement on a purely utilitarian basis and are right not to.

It is not the role of the business case author to coerce decision makers into a utilitarian mode of thought. The objective is to create a rational framework for reaching the best decision, not to eliminate judgement. While most business cases will not carry any great moral significance, the point is equally valid in relation, for example, to the primacy of corporate strategy or mission. A benefits weighting and scoring approach which leaves plenty of room for prioritisation and judgement while still insisting on strict logic in causation and a proper balancing of different factors is much more likely to influence the decision than a determination to give everything a monetary value.

Figure 4.2   Jeremy Bentham and the Department for Transport

anyway, so it is far from clear what is gained by moving what in reality are non-cash benefits into the financial analysis.

STEP 3 – MAP THE OUTPUTS OF THE OPTIONS TO THE BENEFITS OF THE PROJECT

All shortlisted options should deliver good results in terms of the benefits you have now defined. Otherwise why are they on the shortlist? But they will differ in how and how well they deliver them, and it is this which the benefits map needs to tease out.

At this stage, you will need to draw up an outline benefits map, showing the options and the benefits you have specified, and the work still to be done to define outputs and complete the mapping, weighting and scoring. It should look something like Figure 4.3.

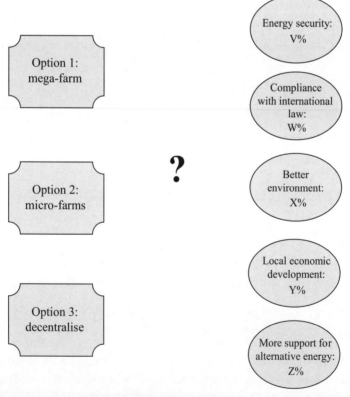

Figure 4.3   Skeleton benefits map

The next step is to establish the outputs of the options. Do this with each option in turn, rather than trying to work back from the benefits. By now you should be quite familiar with each option on the shortlist and will know what it is that each of them is likely to achieve. The challenge is to set them out in sharply defined, observable and measurable terms. Measurable in this context does not necessarily mean quantifiable. Quantification will be delivered by the weighting and scoring process, so it is not essential at this stage. It means simply that there is a reasonably objective way of determining whether the benefit has been delivered, not delivered, or partially delivered. For example, typical benefits of redeveloping an old-fashioned headquarters building might include improved staff morale and more effective networking and teamworking. Typical outputs of the project might include more open-plan working areas and breakout areas and improved cafeteria and exercise facilities for staff. The benefits are essentially unquantifiable, and there is not much mileage in trying to quantify the outputs either, but with reference to the building plans it is entirely possible to say whether a particular option will or will not deliver them, and how well, and to verify that in the evaluation stage.

Common mistakes include:

- Omitting 'static' benefits. A benefit does not have to represent an improvement on the status quo, only an improvement on the implied zero option. For example, if a business case is being made for a fast-growing company to acquire a bigger office, 'Everyone will still have a place to work' is a very important benefit.

- Including legal requirements or other genuinely essential yes/no benefits. All shortlisted options should be delivering these, so they are not going to help with the decision.

- Double counting monetised benefits (see Step 2 above).

- Failing to consult stakeholders (see Step 7 below). Just as you have kept stakeholders engaged through the previous stages of work leading to the identification of options, you should continue to engage them at this stage too, particularly in validating the list of benefits and the connections between outputs and benefits.

Once you have listed all the material outputs of each option and populated the space in the middle of your benefits map, decide which outputs contribute to which benefits. Try not to overcomplicate this by introducing too many outputs or too many gradations of connection. Outputs can contribute to more than one benefit and in some cases you may need to avoid distortions by estimating the percentage to which different outputs contribute to a particular outcome. Do this when it feels intuitively right, but avoid using complexity of arithmetic to put a gloss of objectivity on a subjective judgement. Your benefits map should by now look something like Figure 4.4.

Notice that you do not need to put in a web of criss-crossing arrows between the options and the outputs. The scoring process will take care of that later, and it only creates confusion.

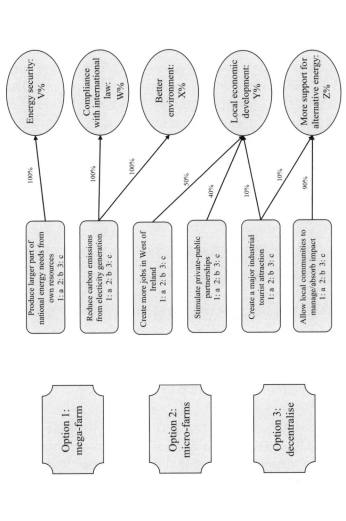

Figure 4.4   Developing benefits map

Option 1: mega-farm

Option 2: micro-farms

Option 3: decentralise

Produce larger part of national energy needs from own resources
1: a 2: b 3: c

Reduce carbon emissions from electicity generation
1: a 2: b 3: c

Create more jobs in West of Ireland
1: a 2: b 3: c

Stimulate private-public partnerships
1: a 2: b 3: c

Create a major industrial tourist attraction
1: a 2: b 3: c

Allow local communities to manage/absorb impact
1: a 2: b 3: c

Energy security: V%

Compliance with international law: W%

Better environment: X%

Local economic development: Y%

More support for alternative energy: Z%

100%

100%

100%

50%

40%

10%

10%

90%

There is proprietary software (ChangeDirector, for example) which will help you prepare a benefits map. Whether you use this is a matter of preference; presentationally it makes life much easier, but it is not essential, and if you do use software tools it is important not to be drawn into over-exploiting the functionality by inputting all sorts of subtle distinctions and cross-connections which make the end result look like the cat got into Grandma's knitting. I have witnessed senior managers, presented with a laboriously prepared benefits map of this nature, declare that the whole approach is a waste of time and it would be better to stop theorising about benefits and get on with the job. This is a pity, as benefits mapping done properly and kept in its place can make a worthwhile contribution to the robustness of the business case.

STEP 4 – WEIGHTING AND SCORING

The next step is to weight the benefits. Which ones really matter? Which are nice to have? This is not a scientific process, so it is best not to agonise too long over the decision, although it is important to ensure that stakeholders recognise and accept the assumptions you have made. Simply divide 100 points between the benefits, regardless of how many there are, to create a percentage weighting factor.

Then score the options in relation to their expected achievement of outputs. Do this out of ten, as a disincentive to drawing inappropriately fine distinctions, and try not to allow fractions or decimals.

Having done this, your map is complete and will look something like Figure 4.5.

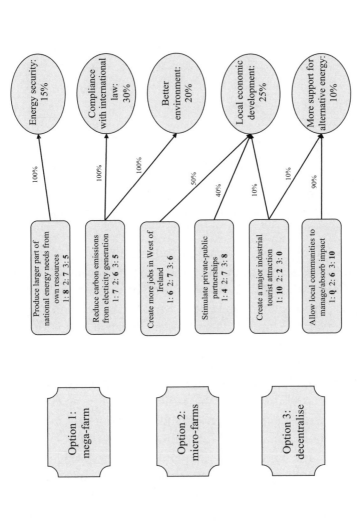

Figure 4.5 Completed benefits map

STEP 5 – REVIEW THE SUBSTANCE

Before going on to complete the calculations, make the most out of the benefits process by standing back from the numbers for a moment and reflecting on the substance of what you have prepared. The following questions may prove very revealing and make as big a contribution to getting the right decision as the whole weighting and scoring process:

- Are there any benefits (it is worth checking the outputs too) which, on further reflection, are so important that the project will be deemed a failure if they are not achieved? If there are, then any option which fails to deliver them, or delivers them only poorly, should be dropped now.

- Do all the benefits really stand in their own right as outcomes which the decision makers accountable for this project, and those to whom they are accountable (taxpayers, shareholders, etc.), would recognise and value? For example, 'improved performance against arrest targets' may be a valid quantifiable output for a policing project, but it is not a legitimate benefit, because taxpayers and members of the community do not care about it. 'Less crime' is. Articulating the benefit correctly gives some protection against distortion and manipulation.

- Are all the causal links valid and true? Go through every link – from option to output and from output to benefit – individually, and test each one both for logic, and for integrity and credibility. This would be a good moment to involve an independent source of advice in the project in a critical friend capacity. If there are grounds for scepticism, revisit it and root out the source of the problem. The benefits of new technology to users and customers are particularly prone to exaggeration.

STEP 6 – RANK THE OPTIONS

Ranking the options is now a simple arithmetical procedure, easily built into a standard spreadsheet. First calculate the weighted value of each output using the formula:

Using the Irish wind farms example, this calculation would be presented as in Table 4.1. To simplify the table, benefits to which no contribution is made are omitted. In a spreadsheet you should include them all to ensure completeness and minimise the risk of error.

Next, calculate the weighted score for each option for each output, using the formula:

The total score for each option is the sum of these weighted scores. Options are then ranked by comparing their aggregate scores. The calculations can be tabulated as in Table 4.2.

The results have to be interpreted intelligently. While the highest scoring option is the best from the perspective of non-financial benefits, it cannot be emphasised enough that this does not even begin to give it the status of the preferred option. No account has yet been taken of disbenefits, financial benefits, costs, or achievability, so there is a long way to go. Moreover, given the inherently subjective and approximate nature of the process, there is no material difference between

Table 4.1   Calculating the weighted value of outputs

Benefit	Weighting	Contribution	Weighted value
Output 1: Produce larger part of national energy needs from own resources			
Energy security	15%	100%	15
Total weighted value			15
Output 2: Reduce carbon emissions from electricity generation			
Compliance with international law	30%	100%	30
Better environment	20%	100%	20
Total weighted value			50
Output 3: Create more jobs in West of Ireland			
Local economic development	25%	50%	12.5
Total weighted value			12.5
Output 4: Stimulate private-public partnerships			
Local economic development	25%	40%	10
Total weighted value			10
Output 5: Create a major industrial tourist attraction			
Local economic development	25%	10%	2.5
Support for alternative energy	10%	10%	1
Total weighted value			3.5
Output 6: Allow local communities to manage/absorb impact			
Support for alternative energy	10%	90%	9
Total weighted value			9
Check – totals should sum to 100			100

Table 4.2   Calculating weighted scores for each option, and ranking options

Option		Output						Total	Rank
		1	2	3	4	5	6		
	Value (from Table 4.1)	15	50	12.5	10	3.5	9		
Option 1	Score	8	7	6	4	10	0		
	Weighted score	120	350	75	40	35	0	620	2
Option 2	Score	7	6	7	7	2	6		
	Weighted score	105	300	87.5	70	7	54	623.5	1
Option 3	Score	5	5	6	8	0	10		
	Weighted score	75	250	75	80	0	90	570	3

Options 1 and 2 as far as the delivery of non-financial benefits is concerned. Nor is Option 3 far behind. The process has, however, already succeeded in teasing out the difficult question which any advocates of Option 3 are going to have to answer – why should we select the option which is least beneficial from the perspective of our most important objectives?

STEP 7 – VALIDATE YOUR WORKINGS WITH STAKEHOLDERS

The subjective character of the judgements involved in identifying benefits, and in weighting and scoring, make it essential to validate all aspects of this process with stakeholders. Exactly how and when to do this depends on the nature of the stakeholder group. If stakeholders are reasonably accessible and prepared to engage in informal workshops, there is a lot to be said for involving them from

Step 1, getting them to identify and own the benefits of the project and explore the relationship between outputs and outcomes. If the key stakeholders are senior decision makers who will be difficult to engage in this way, it may be better to present them formally with your interim conclusions in the course of Step 3 – perhaps showing a simplified benefits map and listing the benefits in order of importance, thus inviting debate at the level of substance rather than methodology. You want stakeholders to tell you about why your assumptions are wrong, not to critique your processes or your numbers.

The process can be tricky if stakeholders divide into camps or are otherwise palpably at odds with each other. People are not usually reluctant to stand where they sit, and it is common enough to find, say, the HR Director and the Finance Director placing radically different values on different types of benefit. Tiresome though this can become, differences of perspective among decision makers are going to have to be confronted at some point, and it can be useful to surface them early and within the context of an estimating process which does give plenty of scope for compromise. In some cases, if consensus is difficult to achieve it may be useful to carry out a simple sensitivity analysis (explained on page 108) on critical weights or scores, to test whether differences of perspective make a material difference to the ranking of options.

It may also help to take stakeholders through a structured interview process where each gives individual weights and scores, so that the ranking of options can be based on averages.

This is labour-intensive, however, and may lead into dangerous territory. Our democratic instincts naturally lead us to count everyone's vote equally, but decision makers are rarely equal, and by doggedly following an apparently democratic process you may inadvertently land the senior decision maker in the position of having to overrule his or her colleagues openly when they would rather have worked through persuasion and influence.

Disbenefits

Projects and programmes always have cash costs; sometimes they also have costs which cannot safely be expressed in monetary terms. These are referred to as disbenefits. Not surprisingly, disbenefits tend to be in the same sort of areas as benefits. Typical disbenefits to consider in a major change programme, for example, would be lower staff morale, or adverse impact on a second-order strategic objective. Disbenefits tend to be fewer in number and narrower in scope, because normally a project is about making investment to achieve benefits, and the disbenefits are incidental. In some circumstances, however, disbenefits can be central. Suppose for some regrettable reason it became necessary to consider a project to tear down all those wind farms you have just built in the West of Ireland – the disbenefits would essentially be the reverse of the benefits listed above.

It is not advisable to try to integrate quantification of disbenefits with quantification of benefits by incorporating negative numbers. Your methodology will almost certainly fall over and no-one will understand what you are trying to do anyway. There are three alternatives:

1. *Offset disbenefits directly against benefits within the scoring process.* This is the simplest approach, but it will only work if benefits and disbenefits are reasonably well correlated. For example, if a disbenefit of wind farms Option 1, the mega-farm, was that n million extra passenger miles would have to be driven each year to get the workforce to the site, thus increasing carbon emissions, this factor could be quantified and, if big enough, taken into account by taking a point off the Option 1 score on the relevant output benefit. If you do this, you must document what you have done.

2. *Do not attempt to quantify disbenefits.* If there are, as will normally be the case, only one or two material disbenefits, perhaps affecting only one or two of the options, then it is probably not worth trying to quantify them. Judgement is already going to be required to compare costings with weighted benefit scores (see below), and adding a third quantitative factor on another different scale into the mix does not necessarily offer any advantage over logging the disbenefits in words. If you do this, make sure disbenefits are not forgotten when it comes to populating the attractiveness-achievability matrix and making the arguments behind it.

3. *Extend the benefits map to the left.* The benefits mapping, weighting and scoring methodology can be repeated for disbenefits, showing disbenefits and outputs to the left of the business case options on the benefits map. This will

only be worth doing if there are numerous and significant disbenefits which cannot be correlated to benefits. If you do this, do not attempt to add benefit and disbenefit scores together as this will have no logical validity.

Conclusion

This chapter has explained how to begin the task of options analysis by assessing the benefits of each option. In order to present decision makers with a clear, rational and accessible basis for comparing different options, you should start working towards plotting the options you have identified on an attractiveness-achievability chart. To get beyond subjective statements which it is impossible to compare, it is important to quantify the benefits of each option.

There are seven steps to quantifying benefits:

1. *Focus on project outcomes.* Articulate the benefits of the project first – not those of each option – in plain language, making use of the work you have already done on drivers.

2. *Exclude money benefits.* Do not count financial benefits. They will feature in the cost model instead.

3. *Map the outputs of the options to the benefits of the project.* Sketch out a benefits map, linking the outputs of each option – its observable, measurable results – to the benefits sought from the project.

4. *Weighting and scoring.* Complete your benefits map by weighting the benefits against each other and scoring the options in relation to their expected achievement of outputs.

5. *Review the substance.* Check to see what your work is telling you. Drop any options which fail to deliver critical benefits. Verify that the project benefits really are final outcomes that stakeholders and customers will value in their own right. Go through all the causal links to see if they are logical and credible. Will your options really deliver the benefits?

6. *Rank the options.* A simple arithmetical procedure then gives you a rank order of the options under consideration. This relates only to non-financial benefits, and does not tell you which should be the preferred option.

7. *Validate your workings with stakeholders.* All the way through this process, make sure that your stakeholders support the assumptions you are making and have had an opportunity to debate the key issues of substance regarding the benefits each option is expected to deliver.

You may then need to carry out an assessment, usually simpler and less formal, of any disbenefits which may arise from one or more options.

Chapter 5 now moves on to how to tackle work on the cost model, which should be proceeding in parallel with work on benefits.

Chapter 4 Exercise: Eastport Pier

The old pier at the seaside town of Eastport suffered severe storm damage in 1987 and has deteriorated to the point where several years ago the sea end of the pier was declared unsafe and closed off permanently. It is an eyesore. Prompted by a local newspaper campaign, council officers have put a lot of fresh effort into soliciting proposals for its revival, and it is approaching decision time. There are three options on the table:

1. *Partial demolition.* The only option that could be afforded completely out of public funds would be to demolish the crumbling sea end of the pier and modify the shore end to make a simple but large, safe viewing platform with picnic benches and fishing places.

2. *Partnership redevelopment.* A local businessman has put together a consortium to lease the pier at a peppercorn rent for 30 years. The consortium would restore the whole pier to a safe condition and there would be public access throughout. A small civic amenity space would be available for community use and the private sector partner would operate a gaming arcade and a large licensed club. Business rates would have to be waived for 15 years. In addition to sourcing the restoration and construction work locally, the consortium would employ about 25 people year round and about 200 part-time seasonal jobs.

3. *Private development.* A Dubai-based company has expressed interest in purchasing the pier outright for a modest sum.

The company would restore the whole pier to its original Victorian condition and build a luxury hotel and restaurant at the sea end. Public access would be restricted to the shore end of the pier, where there would be a number of concessions for local traders and some limited public space for fishing. Specialist contractors would oversee the restoration and development, although there would be some labouring work for locals. The hotel would have about 40 permanent staff, with up to 40 additional jobs in the season.

The Chief Executive of the local authority owns the business case which will be put to councillors for decision. She has asked you to prepare the section on benefits. She has no personal agenda and wants to do and be seen to do the best deal for the community, giving people what they want. Some fairly unstructured survey work has been done among local residents. Forty per cent are retired people, many of whom remember the pier in its heyday of ballroom dancing; their principal concerns are to enjoy the seabirds and the quiet beach front. There is 20 per cent unemployment among those of working age and a growing problem of youth alienation; the stanchions above water are covered in graffiti and beer cans wash around with the tide. Many people commented to the researchers that 'the town needs a life – it's getting down at heel'. Three per cent of those surveyed were keen anglers, all of whom were furious at the closure of the sea end of the pier by 'Health and Safety Nannies'.

Sketch out a simple benefits map, weight and score it, and say what issues of substance you would use it to tease out with key stakeholders. This exercise may well take longer than the others in this book, as you are learning a new methodology, but it will be a worthwhile investment of time before you have to do this for real.

Costs

Own the costings personally. The business case author should be able to explain the derivation of every item in the costing spreadsheet.

Why Costing Goes Wrong

It is unlikely that anyone would be so audacious as to attempt to present a business case without any cost information in it at all, but too often the standard of costing is so poor that it might be better to invite decision makers to have a guess at the costs and form a view on the basis of their own experience. There may be many reasons for this phenomenon, but two stand out as the most likely, and it is worth dwelling on these issues briefly as most of this section is about how to deal with them. Not surprisingly, they recall the two main causes of bad business cases – problems of competence and problems of integrity. The failure to tackle costing with sufficient seriousness and integrity is perhaps the single biggest cause of disaster in projects and programmes. Figure 5.1 gives a grim example.

The first reason why costing goes so badly wrong sometimes is lack of financial and arithmetical competence and confidence. Many otherwise effective managers turn out under pressure to be not particularly numerate and will perpetrate basic arithmetical

The decision to construct a dedicated building to house the new Scottish Parliament was a predictable and understandable consequence of the devolution referendum of 1997. The new Labour Government's White Paper *Scotland's Parliament* asserted that 'the building the Scottish Parliament occupies must be of such a quality, durability and civic importance as to reflect the Parliament's status and operational needs ... an important symbol for Scotland... The objective will be to secure suitable accommodation at a reasonable cost ... Because of the range of sites under consideration and the variety of funding methods potentially available it is necessary to express the cost as a range of between £10m and £40m'.

The estimated cost of the Parliament building at Holyrood rose repeatedly in the course of procurement and construction, and was finally determined in 2004 at £431m, more than ten times the upper end of the range given in 1997. Lord Fraser's detailed report into this fiasco identified many problems, but perhaps none more damning than the failures of costing. There does not appear to have been anything which could properly be called a business case for this massive commitment of public money, despite all the various feasibility studies, design briefs, submissions and so forth. Lord Fraser commented on the brief for the design competition, by which time the 'budget' had become £50m:

The so-called budget, which never had any basis in reality, was not at the time of the design competition set against even the most tentative of cost estimates. (Para 4.49)

This may leave the intelligent observer slack-jawed in horror, but the most important thing for our purposes is to get a little closer to the root of what was not happening in the costing process, so that we can learn from this. The clearest indication is in Lord Fraser's assessment of the state of the budget (then £62m) when the project was handed over to the Scottish Parliament Corporate Body by the Scottish Office in June 1999:

The budgeted construction cost of £62 million was flawed in that:
a. there was inadequate accounting for risk, and the stated budget bore no relationship to a cost plan;
b. there had been a failure to fully appreciate the complexity of the design; and
c. account had not been taken of considerations of blast and security. (Para 9.16)

In other words, the budget had been conceived on a top-down basis, and the detailed costing work to build up a reasonable estimate had not been done. Expert advice had not been sought or taken in areas of costing where it was essential. And note the third point – no-one had done a basic sense check of the cost blocks put into the costing framework, however rudimentary it was, and pointed out that a national parliament (even in the days before 9/11) was going to require additional investment in security infrastructure. Even if your business case is for a lot less than this, aim to do a lot better.

Figure 5.1   Scottish Parliament

errors. An even larger number are incapable of designing a properly functioning, auditable spreadsheet; and the majority will find it difficult to check whether figures put in front of them for inclusion in the business case are actually correct. Complex and sometimes needlessly confusing approaches to figurework imposed by accountants and other experts compound this problem by making even fully numerate managers feel that the calculations are beyond them. Lacking the confidence to challenge or sense-check the emerging conclusions before it is too late, they become inadvertent champions of error.

The second reason is close identification with the project's goals combined with disassociation from its costs. The money to be spent on the project is very rarely that of the business case author and his or her personal interest in it is usually negligible. Having invested energy and enthusiasm in developing the objectives of the project and the best ways of implementing it, the whole business case team is almost bound to have more commitment to seeing the tangible benefits of the project made real than to avoiding a certain quantum of expenditure of somebody else's money. This is particularly evident in the public sector, where even the most public-spirited commitment to saving taxpayers' money can rarely withstand the cynicism induced by witnessing arbitrary central cost-cutting exercises or palpable squandering of resources in other parts of the system. Nor is the private sector immune to the syndrome of business case authors starting from the cost and revenue figures which will yield the required rate of return and working back to the data from there.

The Costing Process

There is no shortcut here. The only way to avoid these problems is to cost the options thoroughly, carefully and honestly, and to engage stakeholders in this part of the business case just as much as in the more relatable parts. Above all, the business case author must take personal responsibility for costs. Many aspects of the work can of course be delegated, but not the overall responsibility. This theme runs right through the following steps to handling costs.

STEP 1 – SET UP THE COSTING FRAMEWORK

It is inevitable that the project sponsor and others will want to know ROM (rough order of magnitude) costs for leading business case options well before it is possible to give them with any confidence. Figures given at this stage do tend to take on a life of their own, and the only defence against this problem is to start even earlier with structured cost analysis, so that at least you understand what the bottom-up process looks like and are better placed to talk down the significance of ballpark estimates. It is easy to seize the initiative in the debate about emerging options by promulgating numbers and it is important that it is the business case team itself which owns those numbers and manages the inevitable movement in them over time.

Structured cost analysis starts with the structure, not the costs. The assumption made here is that cost analysis will be done using a spreadsheet programme, typically Microsoft Excel. Input data may derive from more complex sources, such as econometric or statistical models, or from more basic ones, such as the famous back of an envelope, but a spreadsheet offers the best balance between analytical power and accessibility. There is no better investment of your time in the early stages of the business case process than a short course in Excel. Find a training day, find an e-learning package, find a book, find a coach – but on no account imagine that it does not matter because there is someone else on your team who can do spreadsheets. Personal responsibility for the numbers extends to ownership of the master spreadsheet.

Start by setting up a spreadsheet or worksheet for each option, following the eight top tips in Table 5.1.

Table 5.1   Top Tips for structuring the cost analysis spreadsheet

1	**Keep everything in one spreadsheet**
	There is no one right way to set up the costing spreadsheet, but unless the volume of data makes it impractical it is often helpful to bring all the options into one file and use separate worksheets for each. Often there will be common factors among the options – for example, different organisation restructuring proposals may draw on the same root analysis of payroll costs and the same assumptions about redundancy terms – and keeping everything within the same file makes it easier to operate linking formulas and eliminates the risk of duplicated data getting out of synch.
2	**Label the spreadsheet properly**
	This is as basic as it gets, but it is essential to any chance of the spreadsheet being understood by anyone other than its author. Proper labelling includes: a) an intuitively sensible filename b) version control both in the filename and in a version control worksheet c) headings on each worksheet saying what it is d) generous use of subheadings, and row and column labels so that it is explicit what every series of numbers is doing there e) use of the 'name cell' functionality when one value is applied in various parts of the spreadsheet – e.g. 'inflation factor' or 'contingency'.
3	**Have an assumptions worksheet**
	Assumptions usually contain the key cost drivers, and they must be documented and gathered together in a single list so that they can be readily shared and critiqued. Assumptions should not be relegated to endnotes, but picked out and tabulated separately, giving each assumption a serial number, a short title, and a detailed, quantitative statement.
4	**Document every source and explain every complex formula**
	Either using the 'comment' functionality to associate text with the relevant cell, or making a table of notes, ensure that you state where every value inserted into the spreadsheet comes from, and what every formula is doing if it is not completely transparent. This is essential to making the workings auditable.

Table 5.1 *Concluded*

5	Never overwrite a formula with a value

This is bad practice, and can be compared to laying mines in your own spreadsheet. The absence of the formula is easily forgotten and can damage other calculations and series undetected. The only justification for replacing formulas with values is if a whole data series based on assumptions can be replaced with actuals, and even then it must be done with care to make sure links remain valid, and properly documented.

6	Use borders and shading

The accessibility of a spreadsheet can be immeasurably improved by putting a simple box around the key values, and using colours and lines to emphasise the main messages of the tables. This is really not at all difficult and repays the effort of learning it many times over.

7	Make sure each worksheet will print out sensibly

Some data series are too long to print on a single page, which is OK, but there are few things more irritating for business case users than to be emailed a spreadsheet which prints out as umpteen largely empty pages of apparently unconnected numbers. Use 'set print area', 'print preview' and 'page setup' to make sure each page your file prints out is meaningful, labelled and numbered.

8	If you get help, understand what your helper has done

Experienced business modellers, or even just more IT literate junior staff, can give valuable assistance particularly in enhancing the appearance of spreadsheets and deploying useful but less familiar formulae (such as the IF...THEN function, and LOOKUP tables). This is great, but only if you understand exactly what has been done and know how to amend the input data and the relationships established within the spreadsheet. Good-looking files where changes to prominent data entry 'buttons' produce new answers through unseen workings are temptations to manipulate and best avoided. How do you know they are right anyway?

STEP 2 – IDENTIFY THE COST, SAVINGS, AND REVENUE BLOCKS

The most important part of structuring the cost analysis is to identify the figures you are going to need. What is the composition of the cost of each option? What are the different sources of savings and revenue it could be expected to produce? While this will, of course, be different in every business case, the major cost areas tend to crop up time and again and there are a few common omissions to guard against.

Many organisations, particularly those accustomed to bidding for contracts, will have standard checklists or work breakdown structures which can provide a useful starting point and some protection against omissions. This is also a good stage to seek some informal advice from an individual with relevant experience, since it does not yet matter that they will not be acquainted with the detail of the project and you need not make any great demands on their time.

For a business change project – intended here as a very broad category, encompassing most projects except for construction and engineering projects which of course tend to have rather different headings – the principal cost blocks in your spreadsheet should usually include:

- *IT costs.* If this is going to be a significant component, you must break it down further, for example into hardware, software licences, integration, testing, networking and cabling. Include a line for system support costs for the life of the system.

- *Staff costs and/or savings.* As well as payroll costs/savings, include lines for any one-off costs associated with staff, such as redundancy payments, outplacement services and recruitment costs.

- *Estate costs and/or savings.* Include relocation costs, if any, and any incremental costs for facilities management charges, power, air conditioning, etc.

- *Procurement costs.*

- *Programme/project management costs.* Include consultancy, change management, communications events, etc.

- *Training costs.*

- *Transition costs*, including any parallel running.

- *Contingency.*

This is quite a short list, but will often cover the majority of the items you need to include. Note the importance of looking forward from one-off costs to check if they have a recurring element – IT systems always carry support costs and sometimes refresh costs as well; extra accommodation has an overhead with it. Equally, look backwards from recurring costs to check if they have an investment cost associated with them – staff savings often come with a bill for early retirement or redundancy; outsourcing contract costs also entail a procurement expense to place the contract.

Avoid including more detail than you really need and simply ignore any costs or savings which are not material. Over-intricate analysis runs a big risk of creating confusion, distracting attention from the big issues and increasing the scope for error. If there are complicated areas which are not yet fully understood, such as VAT or other tax issues, goodwill or other accounting issues, or foreign exchange, make a note of them but avoid allowing them to distort the underlying simplicity of the model at this stage.

Consider carefully over what period you should be analysing cost data. This can have a significant impact on net present values and thus on the outcome of investment appraisal. There is no fixed rule for this, but a good guideline is not to go any further into the future than the planning horizon of the organisation unless the analysis is going to be obviously distorted as a result. A typical change programme should be assessed over 3–5 years, as the pace of organisational change tends to preclude much confidence in the long term durability of change. A typical IT project should be assessed over the expected life of the system, which will often be in a similar range. Greater challenges are posed by long-term contracts and by construction projects. It would be madness to cost a nuclear power station development without factoring in decommissioning costs, which will not occur for 30 or 40 years, or to evaluate a 25-year sale and leaseback over 5 years, but it is important not to be drawn into wholly speculative figurework for years in the distant future which has virtually no chance of being right and will never be looked at again. When you have to cost all your options over the very long term (for example, in order to compare the Net Present Value of buying an asset with the NPV of a long sale and leaseback contract), you should only use the figures you absolutely have to and have some confidence in, and keep everything else as neutral as possible.

Most importantly, and recalling the discussion of benefit monetisation above, avoid including 'funny money' unless you have to and if you do, make sure you demarcate it unambiguously from the real thing and try to avoid adding them together. Funny money in this context includes not only inappropriately monetised benefits but also numerous other variants such as expected values of risk, allocated overhead, revaluation premiums and stylised efficiency gains.

Tables 5.2 and 5.3 are real examples of worksheets from a costing spreadsheet designed for a restructuring programme in an actual public sector organisation, amended to protect client anonymity. All the cells in the easy-to-follow summary worksheet were populated by formulae which linked to subsidiary worksheets estimating the costs and savings for each block. These two worksheets were the main ones used in conversations with decision makers.

The most striking thing about these worksheets is their simplicity. A great deal of detailed analysis and some quite complicated calculations lay behind the summary, but these worksheets set out the key financial impacts and the underlying assumptions in a manner which senior staff could quickly understand and challenge.

STEP 3 – POPULATE THE TABLES

Having structured the costing framework, and identified the principal cost blocks, the next step is obviously to populate the tables with numbers. A number of useful tips can be suggested, but there is no substitute for some hard graft at this point. Costing is a relentless, sometimes soul-destroying process and it is important to approach it with determination and to have and to value someone in your team who will count all the beans and count them right. For example, the reliability of the very high level numbers shown in Table 5.2 was dependent on, among other things, the following work:

- line-by-line reconciliation of the computerised payroll with business units' budgeted headcount;

Table 5.2 Cost model case study: summary of option costings

SUMMARY OF COSTS AND SAVINGS

All figures £K	2006–07	2007–08	2008–09	2009–10	2010–11	2011–12	2012–13
Programme costs							
Redundancy	2380	2380	0	0	0	0	0
Transition	300	1300	0	0	0	0	0
Relocation	0	900	0	0	0	0	0
Programme delivery	1000	400	50	0	0	0	0
Total programme costs	**3680**	**4980**	**50**	**0**	**0**	**0**	**0**
Recurring savings							
Estates/facilities management	0	-230	-80	-80	-80	-80	-80
Paybill	-450	-1700	-1743	-1786	-1831	-1876	-1923
General administrative overhead	-45	-170	-174	-179	-183	-188	-192
Total recurring savings	**-495**	**-2100**	**-1997**	**-2045**	**-2094**	**-2144**	**-2196**
Net total financial impact	*3185*	*2880*	*-1947*	*-2045*	*-2094*	*-2144*	*-2196*

Estimated payback period:	5 years
NPV over 5 years @3.5%	-465
NPV over 7 years @3.5%	3,004

Table 5.3   Cost model case study: list of assumptions

ASSUMPTIONS

Serial	Category	Description
1	Redundancy	All surplus posts go at 1/4/07. Posts extended beyond this point count as transition costs.
2	Redundancy	Redundancy costs will divide 50:50 between 06/07 and 07/08.
3	Redundancy	75 per cent of redundant staff will be under 50; 25 per cent over 50.
4	Redundancy	There will be no redundancies at senior executive grades.
5	Redundancy	Redundancy payments will be agreed with Trades Unions at 200 per cent of statutory minima.
6	Redundancy	Redundancies will be abated by staff turnover at 10 per cent per annum.
7	Transition	60 per cent of the paybill saving in 2007–08 is recycled to transition costs.
8	Transition	30 new posts at Grade X are recruited at 1/1/07, and charged to transition costs (see serial 20) for one quarter.
9	Transition	10 per cent of staff made redundant are on gardening leave for half of 2007–08.
10	Relocation	Relocation costs £30K per post regardless of where to/from.
11	Relocation	Only 20 per cent of staff will choose to relocate – others choose redundancy.
12	Relocation	30 per cent of relocation redundancies overlap with restructuring redundancies.
13	Relocation	All staff who decline relocation and voluntary terms are successfully deployed elsewhere in the business.
14	Programme	Recruitment and outplacement services bought in for all new posts and 75 per cent of departing staff.
15	Programme	Contracts for services only; in-house programme team costs are excluded.
16	Estates	Barnsley office is sold for £150K in 2007–08.
17	Estates	Roehampton office lease (£60K) is abandoned in 2007–08.
18	Estates	Facilities management savings of £10K per annum are realised at each abandoned site.
19	Paybill	Paybill costs rise by standardised rate of inflation each year (2.5 per cent).
20	Paybill	All new posts are created at 1/4/07. Posts filled earlier count as transition costs.
21	Paybill	Paybill impacts based on headcount estimates in the business case and 2005–06 payroll data.
22	Paybill	20 per cent of surplus posts are already vacant.
23	General admin	Savings on office costs, expenses etc are estimated at 10 per cent of paybill savings.

- post-by-post assessment of which posts in each business unit were required after the change programme;

- development of a paybill ready reckoner to estimate impact of various options;

- liaison with Human Resources to obtain approximate workforce age profiles;

- research of redundancy package statutory requirements and sector benchmarks;

- market valuation of offices earmarked for disposal;

- market soundings for cost of outplacement and recruitment services;

- market soundings for cost of consultancy support in project and change management;

- discussions with business unit heads on feasible timescales and transition issues.

In another type of project, such as construction or environmental development, the cost blocks would be different, with design, materials, labour, professional fees, transport and so on featuring instead of many of the headings in Table 5.2. The same hard grind of detailed analysis under each heading would still be needed and in that case detailed costings would typically be built up from unit costs within a formal work breakdown structure.

This sort of work is the foundation of a good business case budget. It is not an exact science and one sensible working practice to adopt is to eschew spurious accuracy in budget figures, and indeed to be instinctively suspicious of improbably precise estimates. It is impossible to know that, for example, a proposed new retail outlet will sell 444 units in a week, so if you are provided with a revenue estimate based on that sales forecast, challenge it automatically. Why 444? Has it been carefully chosen to meet the necessary sales target, or does it have some basis in evidence? If it is based on some form of averaging from other outlets, why is that valid? Would it not be more prudent to say 400?

There is a minority tendency among the numerate professions – accountants, economists, statisticians, business modellers, etc. – to look down their noses at this sort of relatively broad-brush approach to costing. This is a big mistake, as it overlooks the absolutely crucial issue of the relationship between the costing process and the decision-making process. Fine-grained models and technical presentations will usually address only a part of the whole picture and can easily be ignored or, worse, provide a false sense of security to decision makers who are actually proceeding on the basis of gut instinct.

Focusing on the big cost blocks and the big numbers has to come first, but there are several areas of complexity which may well need to be addressed soon afterwards. Some are quite technical and it is important to take professional advice, giving professionals a tightly drawn brief and documenting their advice carefully. Common examples include:

- *Tax implications.* What impact will each of the options have on the organisation's tax position? Are capital allowances or other forms of relief available, and do they impact differently on different options? In the context of payments to individuals for whatever purpose, will they be taxable and will there be pressure to gross up? Is VAT recoverable throughout or not?

- *Inflation.* Particularly in times of low inflation, it is usually best to work in constant prices, ignoring inflation altogether. You may need to revisit this assumption, however, if there are good reasons to believe that some costs will inflate at higher rates than others, either because of specific factors such as forthcoming pay settlements or because of sector trend data.

- *Overseas transactions.* What exchange rates should be used in estimating overseas costs and revenues? Where is exchange risk carried? What are the implications of different tax and import/export regimes? Are there any issues with repatriation of profits?

- *Financial accounting issues.* Project investment appraisal should always be conducted in cash terms; sunk costs should be ignored, and accounting entries such as depreciation, impairment and revaluation should not be incorporated into the calculations. Nevertheless, awareness of some financial accounting implications – for example around goodwill in the private sector or capital charges in the public sector – is important and this should be sorted out at an early stage.

- *Management accounting issues.* Should overhead costs be included, and if so at what level? This is often a vexed question, not least because the amounts involved can be large and may affect the outcome of the appraisal. Overhead is rarely just about stationery and train fares and the key questions relate to major items such as accommodation costs, HQ staff costs and IT infrastructure charges. The basic test should be whether the decision the business case is seeking will actually affect these costs or not – are they variable in respect of the action proposed? Do not accept without demur figures based on absorption of fixed overheads. If overhead costs are stepped – for example, if the additional application one of the business case options proposes to run on the corporate IT infrastructure will push the system over the threshold where more air-conditioned space is needed for extra server racks – this needs both professional accounting advice and negotiation with the relevant support areas before anything is incorporated into project costings.

STEP 4 – ADD CONTINGENCY

Contingency needs to be considered in all programme and project costing. To quote the much ridiculed but actually entirely reasonable words of former US Defense Secretary Donald Rumsfeld:

> As we know, there are known knowns. There are
> things we know we know. We also know there
> are known unknowns. That is to say we know

there are some things we do not know. But there
are also unknown unknowns, the ones we don't
know we don't know. (United States Department
of Defense news briefing, 12 February 2002)

Project costing should deal with the costs of the known knowns. Contingency needs to deal with both the known unknowns and the unknown unknowns. The crucial lesson here is that the appropriate level of contingency included within the costings in the business case should comprise both specific provisions for areas of risk within the project and the costings, and a general provision for overruns and unexpected costs.

Specific provisions are best assessed by considering each of the cost blocks in the light of the risks identified in the risk register (see Chapter 6). What would be the cost to the project if a particular risk materialised? Scenario planning (see page 110) can sometimes be useful in this context, providing a structure for analysis of the relationships between different risk factors and their potential impact. Again, it is important to document the assumptions behind the estimation of specific contingency in the same way as every other costing assumption.

General provision can by its nature only be applied as a percentage mark-up. The decisions to be made are to which proportion of the cost to apply it, and how much. Sometimes a straightforward 8–10 per cent on the whole option cost is sensible. It may, however, be unreasonable to apply a general provision to a cost to which a very high degree of confidence already attaches, such as purchase of a known number of off-the-shelf PCs or leasing additional office space, when reliable market quotations have already been obtained. The level of general provision will depend on the type of project, and in particular on the degree of innovation involved.

Government projects in the UK are required to apply contingency in project appraisal in the form of 'optimism bias', a term reflecting observed historical trends of cost underestimation in the public sector. Methodologies and templates are available for estimating optimism bias, which may be helpful, but may also produce results so alarming that they sap any real meaning from the costing endeavour. Optimism bias estimates are routinely in the 30–50 per cent range and can rise as high as 200 per cent. No decision maker would place any credibility in a business case submitted to them with costs which purported to be based on a thorough costing exercise and were then trebled. The Scottish Parliament estimates (Figure 5.1) are best described not as 1000 per cent underestimated, but as plain wrong. As a rule of thumb, a business case should not go forward for decision with an aggregate contingency much larger than 20 per cent. Risks with a catastrophic impact on costs should be treated as risks and prominently flagged for decision makers accordingly, not allowed to distort the presentation of costs.

The appropriate level of contingency is also a function of the relative importance of keeping strictly to budget. If you are faced with a fixed budget – and particularly a fixed, bottom-up budget (see Chapter 2) – the penalties for cost overruns, both for the project and for the business case team, are likely to be much more severe than if the budget is variable, so it makes sense to apply a somewhat more generous contingency. Another important factor is whether the project is intended to generate a profit or surplus, in which case contingency should be set at a higher level. For example, if a new £100m government science laboratory in the end costs £110m to build, that would probably be a relatively acceptable outcome for the customer; but if the laboratory construction had been wholly contracted out for £110m and the contractor had planned in a 10 per cent profit, the error in the project costing would have lost the company its entire margin.

STEP 5 – TEST, DO SENSITIVITY ANALYSIS, AND LOCK DOWN

You have by this stage developed a summary cost model, with more detailed analysis lying behind each cost block, either provided by or validated with the relevant stakeholders and experts, and an appropriate level of specific and general contingency. This is the time to do some *testing*. While you may justifiably not wish to substitute your judgement for that of operational managers and professional advisers, it is important to remember that each one of them has their own tendency towards optimism or (less often) pessimism, their own level of experience and competence, their own prejudices and interests. As one wise project management veteran comments wearily:

It has to be allowed that there is a possibility, however remote, of finding a manager capable of providing estimates that are proved to be consistently accurate when the work actually takes place. This contingency is so remote that it can almost be discounted. When this rare phenomenon does occur it is apt to produce a very unsettling effect on the work-hardened project manager who has, through long experience, learned that it pays always to question every report received and never to take any forecast at its face value. (Dennis Lock, *Project Management*, Gower 2007, p. 67)

In any event, the business case author cannot delegate ownership of the overall cost analysis, and should have the best feel for the contours of the business case options. Sense check the aggregates and sense check every major component of them. Do the costs of each option seem plausible, relative to each other and in the light of experience? Are there any good benchmarks which can be used to assist with sense checking? Test the figures with an independent observer or critical friend to the project – and ask them to audit your master spreadsheet at the same time. Even if this involves paying for a few days of professional services, it is almost certain to repay the investment.

Having tested your figures, you are now ready to carry out *sensitivity analysis*. This is one of those activities which sounds a lot more technical than it really is. There are, of course, contexts in which sensitivity analysis is a complex modelling process in which real skill with mathematics and statistics is required. A business case is not usually one of them. The purpose of sensitivity analysis in this context is to be able to identify for decision makers the variables in the cost model which, if they changed to a certain extent from the central estimate, could alter the recommendation in the business case. This tells them a number of valuable things:

- how marginal the decision is;

- which elements of the case they need to interrogate most closely;

- where there might be particular value in considering changes to the options; and

- which risks need to be looked at most carefully.

For example, if the recommended option in a business case was to relocate head office from London to Leeds and the sensitivity analysis showed that if premises costs in Leeds rose by 3 per cent, then the alternative option of adopting hotdesking and other flexible working practices in London would have a higher NPV, decision makers would be sure to ask some further questions, such as:

- whether the benefits of moving to Leeds identified in the benefits analysis were worth the disruption to operations;

- why the savings from moving out of London were not greater;

- why hotdesking could not be adopted in Leeds; and

- whether a cheaper, non-metropolitan location could be included as a third option.

The risk register in the business case should be populated with reference to specific analysis of the trend in office costs in Leeds, and include a risk that they would rise above trend before new premises could be secured.

In a relatively uncomplicated cost model, sensitivity analysis can be carried out by trial and error. Change some variables and see what happens (but do save the cost model first, and keep the versions you are playing around with clearly labelled in a separate electronic folder). Use common sense – there is no point testing the sensitivity of a redundancy option to paying less than statutory minimum redundancy payments, as no-one is going to accept them. Above all, do not use sensitivity analysis as a cover for laziness in the costings. Showing that a change option becomes less attractive if you need 50 people in the project implementation team instead of 25 is not adding value; instead, analyse the workload properly, state confidently that 30 people will be needed, put a modest element into the specific contingency and do the sensitivity analysis on a variable which is not so easy to forecast or control.

A more sophisticated approach suited to more complex business cases, particularly where there are interdependencies between some of the key variables, is to develop and analyse scenarios. Scenarios are alternative plausible combinations of hypotheses about the future environment, whose potential impacts are evaluated to produce a set of hypothetical outcomes. For example, the return on investment in a new consumer goods manufacturing facility might well be very sensitive both to the input price of steel and to the growth rate in the retail market for the goods in question. One scenario might involve high commodity prices, associated with inflationary pressures, rising interest rates, and recession in major economies. The potential impact of this scenario on both input prices and sales could be estimated, and research done to give at least a broad indication of its likelihood in the relevant time period. If the scenario is considered a 20 per cent risk, and the decision is sensitive to only a marginal adverse change in the two variables, your analysis should give decision makers food for thought.

The final step is to *lock the costings down*. This is easier said than done, as new information and corrections will continue to flow throughout the entire life of the project, but that is precisely why it has to be done. As well as enabling the right decision, the business case document frequently needs to provide an authoritative statement of the project's financial requirements in order to secure funding, and must provide a baseline for measuring project performance and a platform for managing the project (see Figure 1.1 and Chapter 1). It cannot do any of these things if the costings are in a constant state of flux. At a certain point, invariably and rightly dictated by the decision timetable rather than the preferences of the business case author, the case and the costings in it have to be presented as the basis on which the decision is to be made. One year on, the project budget may well look rather different, but it is against this locked down business case cost model that high-level variances will need to be assessed.

Conclusion

This chapter has explained how to create a cost model for the business case. This is an essential part of options analysis, and is often poorly done, with dire consequences. Although expert input is important both in cost estimation and in handling technical issues such as tax, the author of the business case must have a detailed grasp of the cost model and take personal responsibility for it.

There are five steps to preparing the cost model:

1. *Set up the costing framework.* Structuring the cost analysis should start as early as possible. A spreadsheet is usually a sufficiently powerful tool, but you must understand how to use it, and set it up in an accessible and easily auditable manner.

2. *Identify the cost, savings, and revenue blocks.* Begin populating the model by putting in the main cost blocks. Use checklists to make sure you do not omit anything material, paying particular attention to recurring costs imposed by a one-off investment. Keep the analysis as simple as possible.

3. *Populate the tables.* This step is hard work. Thorough research is likely to be needed to obtain market comparators and valuations, HR data, project cost estimates for items such as materials, infrastructure and development, revenue forecasts, etc. You may also need expert advice on accounting issues.

4. *Add contingency.* Include both a specific contingency quantified in the light of the risks specific to each option, and a general contingency to cover unexpected cost pressures.

5. *Test, do sensitivity analysis, and lock down.* Sense check all the figures, and use independent advice to do it again and to audit the master spreadsheet. Use sensitivity analysis – perhaps based on scenarios – to show the impact of

plausible changes to the key variables. Lock the cost model down when you present the business case for decision, as you have then provided the baseline against which future changes must be assessed.

The analysis of benefits and costs completes the work necessary to assess the attractiveness of the business case options. In parallel, however, you also need to be working on achievability, which is the subject of Chapter 6.

Chapter 5 Exercise: Truly Enormous Bank

Truly Enormous Bank plc has a large retail banking presence throughout the UK, with branches in all cities, most major towns, and a certain number of market towns and suburban centres. The branch network is something of a patchwork, a result of years of mergers, closures, openings, and re-organisations. In response to a headquarters campaign to capitalise on national media advertising about the extensive branch network, while improving the revenue generation of each branch, Bob Luster, Area Manager for Derbyshire and Leicestershire, has presented a business case for closing a small branch in Ashby-de-la-Zouch (pop. 12,700) and opening a new one six miles away in Swadlincote, which with its surrounding villages has a larger population of 33,000. This would put it in the third quartile of population centres with a TEB branch. Of the seven major competitors of TEB, three have branches there already. There are other TEB branches in the surrounding major urban centres of Burton (5 miles), Derby (14 miles), and

Tamworth (18 miles). Mr Luster's business case contains the following table:

Table 5.4   Chapter 5 exercise data table

TEB Swadlincote – cost and revenue analysis (£K)					
	2009	2010	2011	2012	2013
Costs					
Premises	-70	-25	-25	-25	-25
Fitting out	-100	0	0	0	0
Communications	-50	-20	0	0	0
Staff	-40	-40	-40	-40	-40
TOTAL	-260	-85	-65	-65	-65
Income					
Account fees	20	50	53	55	58
Attrib. revenue	38	75	79	83	87
Asset sales	180	0	0	0	0
TOTAL	238	125	131	138	145
Net flows	-22	40	66	73	80
NPV	£174K				
Assumptions					
Premises	£45K premium for 10-year lease; £25K annual rent – market tested.				
Fitting out	Standard equipment, benchmarked against most recent openings.				
Communications	Opening ceremony/press event; local advertising in two campaigns.				
Staff	Additional 1 senior supervisor @ £20K salary, 2 cashiers @ £10K to accommodate growth.				
Account fees	Fees based on regional average £40 annual fee income per account.				
Attributable revenue	Based on regional average £3K holding per account and HQ 25 basis points branch revenue attribution formula.				
Account growth	500 new accounts year 1; 500 more in year 2; 5 per cent growth thereafter.				
Asset sales	Agent's estimate for sale price of freehold premises in Ashby.				
NPV	Over 5 years at TEB required 8 per cent discount rate.				

Stephen C Rouge, Head of Retail Network Development, has asked you to take a look at this table. His email to you reads: 'Luster has initiative and I want to give his proposal serious consideration. I have not sent you the rest of the business case, as the strategic arguments prove merely that there is no particular reason not to do what he recommends, and the non-financial benefits are flimsy. The decision turns on the financials. I am meeting Bob tomorrow – please let me know what you think of his presentation and line up the three key challenges which will expose whether he has really done his homework and got his numbers right.'

Assume the arithmetic is correct and the revenue attribution formula and benchmarked figures are accurate. Compose your email to Mr Rouge.

⑥ Achievability

Golden Rule

Advocating a tough, risky option may be the right thing to do. Advocating it without understanding and explaining the risks and practicalities of implementation never is.

To recap briefly, the main purpose of a business case is to recommend a particular course of action for an organisation. So far, we have looked (in Chapter 2) at how to scope the task of writing the business case, preparing the ground so that the objective is clear, the work can be done effectively, and the decision itself taken. Beyond that initial challenge, most of the material in the preceding chapters has really been about the process of determining the best option, the course of action which best fits with the business strategy and which is expected to deliver the greatest benefit in the most cost-effective manner. The plain fact is, however, that if the project fails, its theoretical strategic fit and attractive cost-benefit analysis will count for absolutely nothing. This chapter focuses on achievability. Can the project actually be delivered? How likely is it that the benefits will indeed be realised? After looking at the treatment of risk, and briefly considering implementation planning, the chapter concludes by reviewing the balance between attractiveness and achievability and pulling together the threads of options analysis.

Risk

Risk is a huge subject, on which many books have been written and much complex theory developed. Particularly if technical aspects of risk are in play, or if the organisational culture dictates a modelling approach to risk, there is no alternative to studying this literature. A good introduction is Alan Webb's *The Project Manager's Guide to Handling Risk* (Gower, 2003). The approach to risk in this chapter is non-technical and will not be adequate for the assessment of specialised types of risk, such as safety or environmental risk, or risk in the financial markets. If these are involved, take advice from experts in the relevant field on how to assess them and factor them into the business case.

The good news is that it is not generally necessary to approach risk assessment in the business case with the same degree of attention to detail which the project manager will eventually need to bring to bear. The purpose of assessing risks in this context is not to manage them – although that may be appropriate in some cases and the business case risk register provides the project manager with a valuable starting point – but to factor them into the assessment of the achievability of the project and thus into the business decision.

STEP 1 – SET UP A RISK REGISTER

In the same way as when embarking on the processes for assessing benefits and costs, the first step in the risk assessment process is to structure an appropriate format for capturing risks in a consistent manner. An important difference is that that whereas for benefits you should focus on the benefits of the *project*, and then consider how effective each option is at delivering them, risks should be associated directly with *options* from the outset. This is because all the options should be aiming to achieve broadly the same goals (otherwise they are not commensurate and should be in different business cases), whereas the risks of each option may be completely different. For example, building a brand new eye hospital on a greenfield site, or contracting out ophthalmology services to a group of private clinics, should both generate comparable (though not, of course, identical) benefits in terms of health outcomes for patients and shorter waiting times. But the risks associated with each would be totally different.

The business case risk register spreadsheet should therefore comprise separate worksheets for each option. There is no point making this too complicated, and it will make it easier for decision makers and other stakeholders to absorb if a familiar standard is followed. Structure the register in seven columns: serial, title, description, impact, probability, risk rating and commentary/mitigation (see Table 6.2 on page 125 for an example). Impact and probability should be numerical scores, say from 1 to 10, and risk rating should be the sum of the two. Use colour coding – purple (17 or more, critical), red (14–16, serious), amber (11–13, concerning), green (10 or less, low priority) – to draw attention to the risk rating. This colour coding can be automated in Microsoft Excel using the 'Conditional Formatting' command on the drop down Format menu.

The purpose of the commentary/mitigation column in this widely used format is to document the factors which have been taken into account in assessing the impact and probability ratings. Sometimes the column is simply labelled 'mitigation strategy' and associated with an additional 'risk owner' column to show who can be held to account for taking mitigating action. This is not a mistake, but some care is needed, as the difference in function between a project manager's risk register and a business case author's risk register again comes to the fore. The project manager has to do their utmost to mitigate all the risks and this part of the project manager's risk register must be entirely action oriented. The business case author, in contrast, is quite at liberty to state baldly that a potential risk, if it crystallises, would have a fatal impact on the project or on some aspect of its benefits. The implication, which should be drawn out in the analysis if appropriate, is that the best mitigation strategy for decision makers really worried about this potential risk could be to choose a different option.

STEP 2 – IDENTIFY RISKS FOR EACH OPTION

What are the risks associated with each option? The next step is simply to get together the business case team, brainstorm a list of risks and discuss them. In most cases it is not difficult to come up with a list of risks, by thinking about the assumptions on which the option relies and about what could go wrong. Many risks will be quite obvious and the hard part is to form a balanced and realistic view of how serious they are and how readily they can be tackled. As always with brainstorming, it is a good idea to start off with an inclusive approach. Write down anything which occurs to anyone and then move on to winnow the wheat from the chaff later. The checklist in Table 6.1 might provide some protection against carelessly overlooking a whole area of risk.

It is highly likely that the team will identify a large number of risks associated with each option. Indeed it can often seem

Table 6.1 Checklist of risk areas

Risk area	Risks to consider
Technology	Risk that it will not work, either at all or as well as intended. How complex or novel is the technology involved? Have the required applications run off the planned infrastructure before?
Business process	Risk that developing new processes will take longer and/or consume more resources than expected. Have the necessary business processes already been developed elsewhere, and is there any access to the relevant expertise?
People	Risks associated with staff retention, recruitment, morale and performance. Does the organisation have the skills it needs to implement the project and realise the benefits? Will there be a dip in business performance as a result of staff changes or loss of focus?
Stakeholders	Risk that stakeholders will block or damage this option. What political or industrial relations factors need to be considered? Are there vested interests which may generate active or passive resistance?
Legality	Risk of legal challenge. Particularly if options involve closure of facilities, planning applications, redundancy, relocation, or material changes to staff terms and conditions, legal risks should always feature.
Time/Cost	Risk of estimating errors or overruns. Particularly in areas which sensitivity analysis suggests are important to the business case decision, how likely is it that the basis of the decision will turn out to be flawed?
External	Risk of changes in the wider environment for the decision. Consider political, economic, tax, environmental, planning, and security factors. Is the project controversial, and if so does the organisation have the appetite to sustain implementation when the going gets tough?
Market	Consider competitive and market risks particularly if the project is to create goods or services for sale. Is there a risk that new products or changed market conditions might render your market research invalid by the time your offer is ready?

as if every decision is so fraught with risk that the only safe option is to stay in bed. The next step is to winnow the list.

Winnowing the risk lists is really important. If the risk register is too long, it will lack credibility with decision makers and thus have no influence on the decision. Moreover, if the option goes forward and it is adopted as the project risk register, it will soon become an overgrown weed, diligently cared for by a junior member of the Project Management Office but of no practical use to the project manager. Fortunately winnowing is usually straightforward. Go through the initial list and cut out any candidate risks which are:

- *Too universal.* We do not need to know that the implementation would suffer as a result of a major terrorist incident, for example, unless there is a specific reason to believe that this option is likely to attract terrorist attention.

- *Too vague.* It does not help the decision to have an overarching risk that the cost forecasts are wrong. There have to be specific factors which suggest that significant elements of the costing particular to the option in question are wrong.

- *Self-referential.* While risks relating to stakeholder acceptance – including, for example, the risk of being subsequently overruled by a group board, a senior minister, or a regulatory authority – are entirely valid, risks relating to the business case's own governance and production process are not. 'Board fails to make a decision' and 'business case not produced on time' are process risks for you to manage, not risks which should influence the decision.

- *Too trivial.* Just as with costs and benefits, risks should not feature in the business case if they are not at least to some extent potentially material to the decision. Resist pressure to include trivial risks to appease internal stakeholders – for example, it may be very irritating for the HR team that a certain option might require newly written HR procedures to be put in the bin, but should it really affect the decision? That is the only test which matters.

- *Costs in disguise.* One of the more devious tricks used in misleading business cases (see Figure 1.2) is to underestimate costs and use the risk register to cover your back. Any candidate risk such as 'not enough software licences purchased' or 'redundancy payments larger than anticipated' should ring alarm bells. Generally such figures should be known with some confidence and any identified uncertainties covered by specific contingency in the costings. Use the risk register only where there are hard-to-quantify downside risks which there is not enough information to cover in contingency; an example might be a case where the need for secrecy has prevented reliable market soundings ahead of a production or procurement decision.

- *Disbenefits in disguise.* 'Cutting pay by 15 per cent may cause retention problems and lower staff morale' is a typical example. This is a certainty, not a risk, and should be considered as a disbenefit in the benefits analysis.

STEP 3 – MITIGATE THE RISKS AND POPULATE THE REGISTER

The brainstorming and winnowing process should have left you with a reasonable list of risks for each option. The next step is to fill in the register constructed at Step 1, documenting and, where appropriate, initiating relevant mitigating action at the same time. The best way to approach risk scoring is to start with an assessment of impact and probability in the absence of any mitigating action and then moderate it in the light of whatever mitigation you are able to propose. If a risk could have a fatal impact on the project and seems quite likely to come to pass, start by scoring it at impact 10 and probability 8, giving a raw risk rating of 18, a critical risk. If on consideration there are practical steps which could be taken to deflect part of the impact and to isolate and deal with the potential causes, the scores could be reduced to 8 and 6, giving an adjusted risk rating of 14, at the low end of red.

For example, if in the opinion of technical advisors there is a significant risk that the system architecture envisaged in one option will not be stable, this could easily be a critical risk. If a risk reduction phase can be incorporated at an early stage into the project plan and a viable contingency plan agreed, this would reduce the impact score and might bring the risk rating down to red. The condition should be noted in the commentary column and highlighted in the analysis. You must also take, or at least plan for, the relevant mitigating action. This is not a paper process. In this example, detailed planning and initiation of the proposed technical risk reduction phase would be a task for the project manager once a decision has been taken, but the business case author must have established that including a risk reduction phase is a viable approach, and confirmed an outline cost and duration with expert stakeholders.

A typical business case risk register, adapted from an actual business case, is shown in Table 6.2.

Table 6.2   Risk Register case study: An option to develop a secure communications system for an international organisation

No.	Risk title	Description	Impact	Prob	Rating	Commentary/ Mitigation
1	Bandwidth	Bandwidth limitations in some of the international connections may cause unacceptably slow system performance.	8	7	15 (Red)	Broadening bandwidth to allow statistically validated user acceptable response times would be prohibitively expensive in parts of Africa and Central Asia. A study on the scope for selective stripping down of functionality for affected locations is under way.
2	Office-based working	The system cannot be made secure to use on handheld devices, so to realise the benefits fully we will have to contain the trend of users working increasingly away from the office. This may be unachievable.	6	9	15 (Red)	Major business change risk. Work to develop a stronger data security culture and protocols to allow limited interface with the non-secure email system may ameliorate, but will not solve, the problem.
3	Technical architecture	The system design relies on an integration of new commercial off-the-shelf applications whose claimed compatibility has not yet been tested in a live environment.	10	3	13 (Amber)	While this would be a fatal outcome, the demonstrator project is going very well and full results will be available prior to the investment decision.
4	Data protection	Legal advisers have suggested that international transmission of some personal data held on the system may breach data protection laws in some jurisdictions.	5	6	11 (Amber)	Further advice is being sought from Counsel. The impact would be to exclude certain datasets from the shared areas, which would be frustrating for users.

Table 6.2   *Concluded*

5	Physical security	Security authorities may require costly structural changes to the building in which the servers are to be based.	8	5	13 (Amber)	Altering the fabric to improve security will cause planning difficulties, and it is not clear where the funding would be found. Discussions with security authorities are continuing.
6	User interface	Standardisation and cost control will require some familiar and valued features of the legacy system user interface to be discarded, which may cause user acceptance problems.	5	4	9 (Green)	The user interface development team is optimistic that modifications to the proposed interface in the light of user feedback will deliver 80% of the valued features.
7	Selective rollout	Affordability constraints mean that offices in some countries will not be connected for some years, which may lead to internal conflict over rollout priorities and alienation of those not prioritised for a secure connection.	5	5	10 (Green)	A transition risk. We are engaging operational management in confirming the priority listing, and a plan to provide extra support to those not initially selected is being developed.

In reality the register was considerably longer, comprising nearly 30 risks, which in retrospect made it too unwieldy. The preferred option, for which this was the risk register, was adopted and as the project unfolded it became apparent several months down the line that Risk 5 on this list was in fact the critical one. Resolving it caused major delays to the project as stakeholders wrangled over cost sharing and attempted to revisit the requirement to deal with the problem. It would have been better for the risk to have been assessed as red or purple, highlighted more prominently in a shorter list and targeted for intensive mitigating action before a decision was made. This is a good example of why a business case risk register needs to be succinct and tightly prioritised, while a project manager's risk register, with a different purpose and a different audience, needs to be comprehensive.

STEP 4 – EVALUATE EACH OPTION'S RISK PROFILE

The final step is to stand back from the risk register you have created for each option and prepare a candid assessment of its overall risk profile. This is not just a matter of summarising eloquently the commentary in the register. Considerable thought needs to go into this assessment, as it should clarify for decision makers the true nature of the risk they would be taking on and enable them to take a considered view of their appetite for risk in the context of the project. The evaluation of option risk profiles should be based on three factors: the overall level of risk, the timing of risks and mitigating actions, and a comparison with other shortlisted options.

Overall level of risk   It is important to be bold enough, when supported by robust risk analysis validated with stakeholders, to assert that a particular option is *too risky*. Decision makers are free to override this judgement, but it is an entirely appropriate recommendation in a business case to argue that, despite the many attractions of an option, the purple and red hues of the risk register are too deep, or one particular critical risk too hard to mitigate, and it should be rejected on risk grounds alone. This recommendation would need to take due account of the organisation's appetite for risk and the consequences of failure. If all the options appear to have a highly adverse risk profile, some serious reconsideration of the case for change and the suite of options identified is needed.

Timing of risks   Often options will have different risk profiles *over time*. For example, if two options are more or less equally risky at first draft stage, it may be the case that by the time of the decision vigorous mitigating actions have largely eliminated the major risks in one, while little can be done to improve the other until the investment is already committed and implementation under way. This is particularly important if, as is often the case, the business case goes through a number of iterations before being finally presented for decision. For example, if an outline business case shows that one option is significantly ahead of the others, but will only be viable if a particular business partner chooses to participate, it is obviously a high-risk option, but it would be too crude simply to mark down its achievability for that reason. Instead, decision makers will expect you to pull out all the stops to make sure those negotiations have reached agreement in principle before they have to make their final decision.

Comparative analysis   In order to be able to plot the options on the attractiveness-achievability chart, the risks of each option must be assessed *relative to each other*. The length of the risk register is almost never a good guide to this, but a count of purple and red risks at least offers a starting point. While avoiding any pretensions to scientific method, it would be reasonable to suggest that an option facing three critical risks was less likely to be achievable than an option facing none. Relative positioning on the chart needs to be accompanied by an appropriately nuanced commentary, distinguishing between the different types of risk and mitigation affecting different options. Some risks are impossible or very difficult to mitigate, while others may be susceptible to complex, expensive mitigation effort. Some risks are relatively predictable, others essentially random. Some options carry a small risk of total failure, others a higher risk of mediocrity. These differences frame choices for decision makers and the role of the business case is to make them explicit, securing informed acceptance of the risks as an inevitable part of the decision and the project.

Implementation Planning

The assessment of the achievability of each option will also be facilitated by carrying out some preliminary implementation planning. Very similar considerations to those discussed in relation to risk should govern your approach to the planning exercise, namely:

- each option needs its own plan, for purposes of comparison;

- the purpose of the plan is to inform the business case decision;

- the level of detail and complexity needed will be largely driven by the culture of the organisation and the expectations of decision makers;

- the plan gives the project manager a starting point, but in no way does their job for them.

In the final version of the business case it may well be appropriate to develop the implementation plan for the preferred option in more detail, to give decision makers greater confidence in the achievability assessment and to give the project manager a better headstart.

The amount of effort which needs to be assigned to implementation planning in the business case depends on the nature of the project. In some projects, such as all those related to preparation for the Olympic Games, time is absolutely critical, and the same degree of rigour which has to be applied to costing should also be applied to planning. Indeed many of the disciplines are comparable – setting up the planning structure, identifying the main time blocks, populating the plan by researching the detail of every line item, adding contingency, testing and carrying out sensitivity analysis. For other, less time-critical projects, plans are important principally as a tool of cost estimation and as an indicator of project completion dates, and are less likely to interest decision makers in their own right.

For time-critical projects, and also for all engineering and construction projects, it is essential to be able to call on the services of a professional project manager experienced in the use of appropriate proprietary planning software such as Microsoft Project to develop detailed Gantt charts allowing for resource planning and critical path analysis. For a more broadly-based business decision, this level of specialist support is probably not necessary, and if you as the business case author are not a trained project manager (and you do not need to be), you will probably find this sort of approach and this sort of software over-engineered and unhelpful.

In most cases, following your instincts and staying within your abilities and experience will work out fine, so long as two cardinal principles are respected. The first is that there must be a timeline, both narrated in text and graphically represented. Decision makers need to know when the project will deliver, and when the benefits will be realised, and this duration estimate must be built up from timed activity blocks just as the cost estimate must be built up from cost blocks. These timed activity blocks have to be shown graphically so that readers can, for example, quickly grasp the scale of parallel effort required to meet an aggressive project end date, or readily see and question surprisingly long or short durations for particular activities.

The second cardinal principle, again echoing good practice in costing, is that the implementation plan and its component parts must be transparently documented, sense checked and validated with stakeholders. Over-aggressive estimates for delivery timescales are just as common as serious underestimation of costs and can also have serious consequences. There is frequently a connection between the two. Robust scrutiny of the plan therefore provides a valuable cross-check on the costings. For example, if a milestone such as 'new staff in post' is not preceded by a substantial time block for recruitment activity, you need not only to amend the plan but also to check that the costs of recruitment have been included. Again, if technical advisers reviewing the draft implementation plan for one option recommend another month for user acceptance testing, that not only adds a month to the project duration but also adds a month of fees/salaries and overhead for the testing team and the project team.

If constructed following these principles, even a high-level implementation plan can serve as a valuable bridge between the inevitably aspirational world of strategy and benefits mapping and the hard reality of making the option work on the ground. A good plan – intelligently interpreted – can add significantly to decision makers' levels of confidence (or anxiety, as appropriate) about the practical achievability of an option.

Concluding the Options Analysis

Pulling together the strands of the options analysis is done by plotting each option on the attractiveness-achievability chart, and then adding sensitivity analysis to the resulting presentation.

PLOTTING THE CHART

While plotting the chart is not a scientific process, nor is it a matter of guesswork. By now you have available:

- benefits scores;

- net present values;

- relative risk assessments; and

- estimated completion dates.

All this data supports the composition of the chart. Options with higher benefits scores and higher NPVs will be higher on the chart. Options with more favourable risk assessments and earlier implementation dates will be further to the right on the chart. Where costs and benefits point in different directions, or risk profiles are hard to compare, options should be plotted close together, accurately representing the difficulty of the decision. Once all the options have been plotted, it is possible to draw two tentative, unproven conclusions from the presentation.

The first conclusion is that options plotted to the left of *and* below any one other option are *dominated*, and cannot be the preferred option if the chart is considered robust. This is because they are both less attractive and less achievable than at least one other option, so why would they be chosen? In Figure 6.1, Options 3 and 4 are dominated by Options 2 and 5 respectively.

The second is that the most likely candidate for preferred option is that nearest to the top right of the chart, although because more balanced options are generally preferable it is a good idea to draw a curved attractiveness-achievability frontier (see Figure 6.1). There may well be more than one option lying on or close to the frontier and it is unwise to lean too heavily on fine distinctions. The right approach is to harness the presentation to frame the issues for decision makers and assist them in dealing with the substantive conclusions of your analysis. For example, in Figure 6.1, it may be that a naturally cautious group of decision makers instinctively want to choose Option 1. The attractiveness-achievability chart

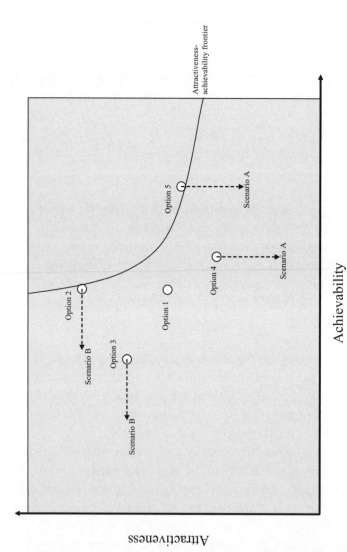

Figure 6.1   Completed attractiveness-achievability chart

does not prove them wrong. But it insists that they question and justify their instincts. Do they not believe that Option 2 is more attractive? Which part of the costings or the benefits analysis do they not accept? Do they not care that Option 5 is more achievable? Are they accepting the risks of Option 1 with open eyes?

ADDING SENSITIVITY ANALYSIS

You carried out sensitivity analysis as part of the work on the costings (see pages 108–111 in Chapter 5), and it is important that the conclusions you reached at that stage feature prominently in this overall presentation of the options analysis.

There are different approaches possible to representing the results of sensitivity analysis in the business case. An established management accountancy approach would be to use expected value analysis, which produces an adjusted forecast by multiplying the results of different scenarios by their percentage probability and taking an average. This will rarely work in business cases, both because it relies too heavily on inevitably speculative quantification of risk, and because it does something of a disservice to the nature of enterprise. If decision makers want to take a big risk to win a big prize, it is not your role to hide either the risks or the prize in a humdrum average which conceals an all-or-nothing reality.

A more practical approach, which utilises your judgement as business case author but exposes it to the challenge of decision makers, is to reflect the principal sensitivities on the attractiveness-achievability chart, and discuss them in the accompanying text. In Figure 6.1, the result of Scenario A coming to pass is that Options 4 and 5 become less attractive – either because of rising costs or falling benefits or both – while Scenario B makes Options 2 and 3 less achievable – perhaps because of more serious obstacles or delays to implementation. Clearly, decision makers must look hard at these scenarios and sensitivities as they have major implications for the selection of the preferred option.

Conclusion

This chapter has explained how to complete the options analysis by assessing the risks associated with each option, carrying out preliminary implementation planning, and populating the attractiveness-achievability chart.

Risk is a particularly important factor in decision making, and for purposes of most business cases is best tackled in four steps:

1. *Set up a risk register.* Each option should have a separate risk register, with numerical assessment of the probability of each significant risk occurring and of the impact if it did.

2. *Identify risks for each option.* Brainstorm a long list of risks, using checklists to ensure you do not miss anything, then winnow out universal, vague, trivial, or purely internal risks, and those which would be better expressed as costs or disbenefits.

3. *Mitigate the risks and populate the register.* Consider where it is possible to reduce the probability or impact of each

risk, and take this into account when scoring risks and populating the register. Decision makers will only look at the top few risks, so make sure they are the right ones and keep it short. You are not constructing the project manager's comprehensive risk register.

4. *Evaluate each option's risk profile.* Assess the risk profiles of the business case options and compare them. Decision makers will need your advice on which risks can be mitigated more effectively and reliably than others, and when, and on which options might simply be too risky to take forward.

Implementation planning is an important aid to costing, and may also provide a strong indicator of achievability in its own right. For time-critical projects, over-aggressive implementation planning is a serious danger, and you may need professional project planning support. In all cases you need to show decision makers a realistic timetable and an estimated date for project completion.

Bringing all the work of options analysis in Chapters 4, 5 and 6 together is best done through the attractiveness-achievability chart. You are now in a position to plot the different options on it and to judge which appear to offer the best balance between the desire to maximise value for money and the imperative of completing the project successfully and in time.

As a business case author, the job of options analysis is done when decision makers have a thoroughly researched and tested, well presented document which makes them confront the full range of issues explicitly and take responsibility for their informed decision.

Chapter 6 Exercise: Power Station in Space

Following the collapse of the ill-fated West of Ireland wind farm project, the Government has been urgently exploring alternative solutions to the long-term requirement for more, greener energy. A business case is in preparation with a range of options. Option 1 is to participate in a new European Space Agency project, which is being heavily promoted by the European Commission, to build a European power station in space to harvest solar energy. A five-year development phase is proposed, focusing primarily on resolving issues in energy storage and transmission, after which the station would be constructed over seven years by a multinational team using NASA shuttle transport.

Although hugely expensive, the cost-benefit analysis suggests that no other option is as attractive over the long term (40 years). The project is attracting considerable press attention and political comment, both positive and negative. At the moment seven EU member states have signed up and negotiations on cost sharing and work sharing are in progress.

The business case author has asked you to comment on the achievability of Option 1. Prepare a risk register, with at least five risks of different degrees of gravity, and a paragraph of preliminary comment on achievability. Feel free to make up plausible facts if it helps illustrate your points.

⑦ Winning the Argument

Golden Rule

Methodical stakeholder management will only work if you also bring the leadership and positive emotional energy needed to carry the team and the wider community through to the right decision.

Chapter 1 was about preparing the ground for a successful business case. Chapters 2–6 were about building the framework and the substance of the argument for the best course of action. In Chapter 8 we will look briefly at pulling it all together, but in truth if you have reached this point the heart of the business case should be already there. All this good work will, however, count for absolutely nothing unless in parallel you have carried the people involved along with you. Making the case is not enough. You need to listen to your stakeholders, understand and act on their concerns, and win the argument.

Winning the argument is a continuous process which begins on the day the business case is commissioned and ends only when the whole endeavour is transferred to the project manager's communications workstream. It is considered here in three parts (running alongside each other, not in sequence): stakeholder mapping, which provides the framework for action; communications, which provides the approach; and leadership, which drives the whole process. The totality can be referred to as stakeholder management, but this needs to be broken down as the term is too all-embracing.

Stakeholder Mapping

The purpose of stakeholder mapping is to provide the framework for winning the argument by identifying who the stakeholders are and categorising them for targeting. Identifying stakeholders should not normally be particularly difficult. The main temptation to resist is to make the list too long. It is too long if it extends beyond the business case team's realistic capacity to engage and communicate. If this is a danger, try restructuring parts of the list into stakeholder groups.

For example, Table 7.1 is a list of stakeholders in a possible project to re-engineer the supply chain for an armoured vehicle.

Not all these people will be engaged in the decision on the business case, and some may have very little if any influence on it, but all have a stake in the outcome.

It is conventional, and good practice, to map stakeholders from such a list on to a two-by-two matrix, where their relative power (understood as their capacity to influence the decision) is measured along one axis and their relative stake (the potential impact of the decision on their interests) is measured along the other. The placement of stakeholders and stakeholder groups on the map gives a general indication of the best management approach. Figure 7.1 provides a template.

Tell Starting at the bottom left of the grid, it is important not to devote too much precious resource to engaging

Table 7.1   Example list of project stakeholders

Armoured vehicle maintenance project – stakeholders
Head of Logistics Command
Army Chief of Staff
Head of Frontline Command
Deputy Head of Logistics Command
Chief of Procurement
Chief Executive, third line maintenance agency
Operations Manager, third line maintenance agency
Commercial Director, third line maintenance agency
Defence Finance Director
Defence Efficiency Project Director
Chief Executive, original equipment manufacturer
Minister of Defence
Commanders of infantry regiments
Field engineers
Infantry troops
Families of infantry troops
Parliamentary Defence Committee
Small and medium enterprises in the supply chain

stakeholders whose stake in the decision is not that great and who have relatively little influence on it. Stakeholders here are often larger groups, such as the general public, junior staff not directly affected by the project, or non-business critical suppliers and subcontractors.

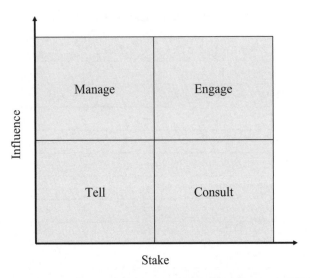

Figure 7.1   Stakeholder mapping template

Consult   At the bottom right, stakeholders who have a significant stake in the outcome but can do little to affect the decision are sometimes neglected in order to focus on cultivating decision makers, but that is unwise. Sensible decision makers will want to know that such stakeholders have been consulted so that the impact on their interests is properly reflected in the options analysis; and the project manager and the organisation may reap a bitter harvest if the seeds of resistance and disengagement are sown at this stage. Stakeholders here tend to be directly affected groups, such as staff whose jobs are to be significantly changed or moved, service users, or local communities.

Manage   At the top left lies the most dangerous category, stakeholders who have significant influence on the decision but will feel its impact to only a limited extent. They are dangerous because they may destabilise or even halt the project without ever fully engaging with the emerging business case, perhaps because of its impact on other projects in the context of organisational politics or resource allocation, or at worst simply as a demonstration of power. These stakeholders tend to be influential individuals, such as the Chief Executive or Chief Finance Officer (if not close to the project), particular non-executive directors, or, in a governmental context, ministers or councillors.

Engage At the top right of the grid are the stakeholders who will shape and make the decision. It is primarily to them that the business case is addressed, and in most cases they must be brought along on the business case journey, not just presented with a document at the end. As well as the formal decision makers, this group may well include key suppliers or customers.

For example, a map of the stakeholders for the armoured vehicle project listed in Table 7.1 might look like Figure 7.2.

Clearly in this instance, as is usually the case, stakeholders are widely dispersed around the grid, and a differentiated communications strategy will need to be adopted.

Communications

Once the stakeholders have been mapped, the next step is to determine the communications strategy. Communications is a professional discipline in its own right and a substantial project

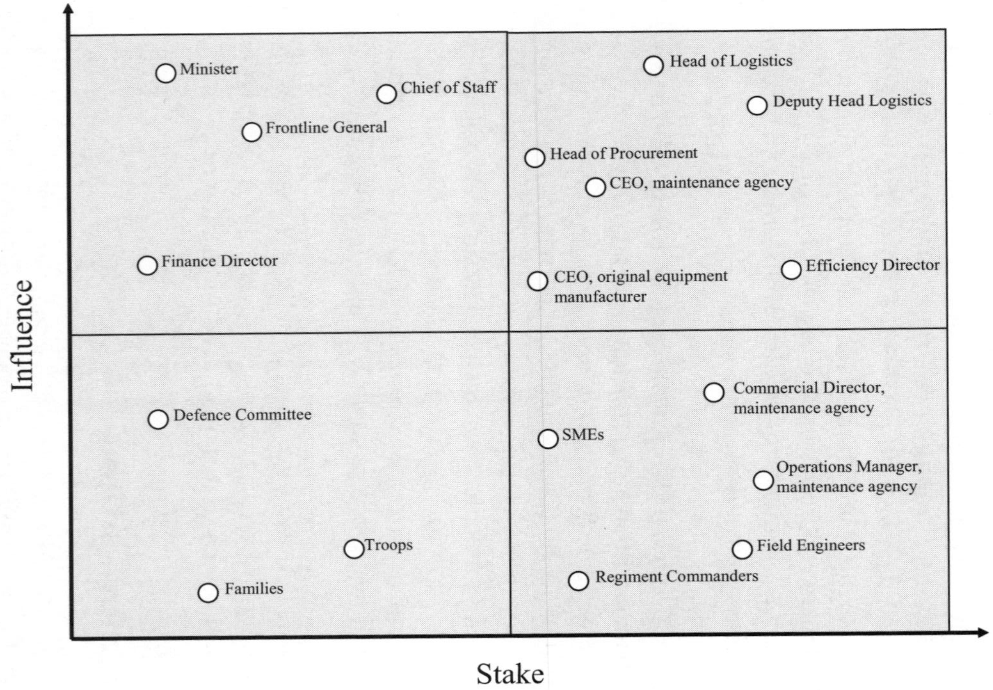

Figure 7.2   Example stakeholder map

affecting large numbers of people is likely to need dedicated professional communications support as early as the business case stage. Even for smaller projects, you would do well to seek expert advice and support, as amateurism in this area can rebound badly. In all cases it is important to make full use of existing communications channels and mechanisms, internal and (where appropriate) external. Establishing relationships and networks in which people will engage, and establishing media vehicles (whether websites, blogs, newsletters, corporate events, or just circular emails) to which people will actually pay any attention takes a considerable investment of time and money. If the organisation has already made such investments, use them.

Which tools to use, then, and in what way should the communications strategy be differentiated in response to the differentiation in the stakeholder map? A '4+1' approach can be adopted, deploying the communications toolkit to meet the needs of each of the four segments of the grid, plus one further important group – the business case team itself.

TELLING

Communications to stakeholders in the 'tell' segment must make limited demands on both the producer and the consumer, otherwise you will be wasting scarce resources and they will not listen. Communications will generally be one-way only. Depending on the size of the groups and whether they are internal or external to the organisation, and on the resources available to the team and proportionate to the scale and profile of the project, options to consider include information bulletins, features placed or blogs written in house magazines and websites, slots in scheduled corporate events, articles placed in professional journals and media interviews.

In all cases it is imperative to start from the needs and interests of the audience, not those of the project. What are they likely to be curious about? What is their stake (however modest)? Abstract argument rarely convinces or even registers through such channels; focus rather on what will be tangibly different. Framing this sort of short, wide circulation communication can be salutary for the development of thinking in the business case, forcing the team to articulate the objectives and benefits of the project sharply and in plain English. In contrast, it is not usually prudent to use this sort of communication to ruminate publicly on the merits of alternative options, as at worst such exposure could put certain options in jeopardy and at best it is disingenuously inviting engagement you do not really want and complicating subsequent communication about the eventual decision.

CONSULTING

Most of these considerations apply equally to communications with stakeholders in the 'consult' segment. The vital additional factor is that at least some of the channels opened must incorporate a feedback process which enables the business case team to capture the views of these stakeholders. Since few things are more guaranteed to antagonise than a charade of consultation, it is essential to decide at the outset on which aspects of the business case you are genuinely interested in the views of these stakeholders. In the armoured vehicle maintenance example, for instance, decision makers need to know what field engineers think about the quality of spare parts supplied to the front line and the potential value of secure online technical help; they are very unlikely to care what the engineers feel about whether their military colleagues or a private sector company should carry out third line repairs. So consult them about one and not the other.

It may or may not be practical to consult stakeholders in this category individually. If it is not, both qualitative and quantitative methods of consultation should be considered. Quantitative evidence – such as '90 per cent of regiment commanders say that delays in the supply chain for armoured vehicle spares are affecting operations' – can be a compelling addition to the business case, but bear in mind that collecting it is not usually perceived as consultation and will not in itself help with stakeholder management. Qualitative engagement such as focus groups can provide valuable texture to the feedback, and when communicated back to the wider group in conjunction with quantitative data can strengthen the emerging story of the business case and begin to build positive attitudes.

MANAGING AND ENGAGING

For the 'manage' and 'engage' segments, individual communication is a prerequisite for success. Powerful people tend to be busy and it is a beginner's error to expect that they will devote time to reading lengthy drafts or general communications material. Note that senior stakeholders in the 'manage' segment will give the business case least time of all, as higher priorities will crowd it out. Messages will need to be very short and individually tailored to their interest in the project. Do not invite these people to workshops. Request a personal interview early, to demonstrate willingness to listen and to establish first hand their interests in and views on the project and its objectives. If these can be adequately reflected in the shaping of the preferred option, future communication can take the form of very succinct briefing through whatever channels they prefer. If the initial interview suggests that they are going to be unhappy with the preferred option, action to manage the problem is essential. Forms of words will not work, as they will not be reading them. Instead, informal interventions from, typically, the business case sponsor are needed to pinpoint the specific concessions necessary to avert a veto and to create a climate of cooperation.

The only difference in the communications strategy best adopted for stakeholders in the 'engage' segment is that they can reasonably be expected to have a greater tolerance for meetings and a greater appetite for papers on the subject. Individual pre-positioning meetings prior to meetings of whatever board or other senior governance body has decision-making authority over the business case offer a really important opportunity to avoid surprises, and to ensure that you understand any individual concerns and priorities which may not necessarily be aired in open forum. In many cases it can be an excellent tactic to engage stakeholders in this segment in the business case from an early stage by inviting them to join the Design Board (see Figure 2.2). Be careful, however, not to create a circle of enthusiasts and leave dissenting forces to gather outside the laager.

Stakeholders in the top right part of the map tend to be highly sensitive to any possibility that the team may be keeping them in the dark, so it is important to maintain a flow of information and reporting which is at or even marginally beyond their absorptive capacity. So long as an executive summary is provided, there is nothing wrong with sending stakeholders in this group dense analytical documents which they are in practice unlikely to read. They may pick up something in their particular area of interest which you would otherwise have missed, and in any event you will have done what you can to include them. What is not acceptable, however, is sending barrages of documents (especially as email attachments) whose inter-relationship is not clear, which leave senior people at risk of commenting on an out-of-date version, which lack a summary, or which they are supposed to read in an unreasonably short time before a meeting.

COMMUNICATIONS WITHIN THE TEAM

Finally, do not neglect communications within the business case team itself. As business case author, you are also a team leader, and need to carry the team with you on the journey towards completion and decision. Even in a small team, information inequalities can build up surprisingly quickly, and people can easily become demotivated if, for example, they find they have spent many hours preparing a cost model for an option which has been fundamentally modified without their knowledge, or crafting a delicate communication for a staff update which the sponsor has already decided to cancel. Poor communication within the team can have immediate adverse external impact as well. Stakeholders will not appreciate receiving one call from the team about their views on human resource implications, and another to invite them to a benefits mapping workshop, or seeing back-to-back meetings in their diary on what for them is the same topic.

Tactics will depend very much on team size, and on to what extent the team are working full-time or part-time on the business case. At a minimum, you need to establish and agree up front:

- a regular update process – normally through periodic team meetings, perhaps even daily if the pace is particularly fast;

- a protocol for stakeholder engagement – who is authorised to approach whom;

- a process for communicating the results of key meetings – how will you update the team on your meetings with the sponsor, or governing body meetings;

- a process for recording stakeholder feedback – everyone who sees stakeholders must communicate their feedback promptly to the whole team, and a record needs to be kept;

- a document management and version control process – how will the team use the available document management technology, who owns which documents;

- a records management protocol – who has the task of maintaining file structures.

Leadership

The journey from the mandate to produce a business case to the eventual decision is a voyage through narrow straits and treacherous waters, for which the practical guidance in this book aims to offer some navigational skills. It is also an emotional journey, a real sea voyage, and technical skill alone will not get you through it. Both the business case team itself, including the sponsor and those decision makers who are closest to the project, and the wider stakeholder community are on this journey with you, and it is incumbent on you personally to produce and sustain the positive emotional energy and commitment which will carry everyone through to the end. All the most successful business case authors are able to provide this kind of leadership to one degree or another.

Consider the emotional journey of the team and the broader constituency which are directly involved in the business case and want it to succeed. It looks something like Figure 7.3.

This characteristic pattern resembles and runs in parallel with the familiar 'Forming-Storming-Norming-Performing' pattern of team dynamics, but it relates directly to the nature of the work on the business case. After an initial burst of enthusiasm, the realisation of the scale of the challenge and the virtual impossibility of producing meaningful data and analysis in the time available tends to drag the whole team down towards despairing that the business case can ever be accomplished successfully. Pulling them through this, and rallying the determination to grind through the tough issues and get to a position of confident control over the end product, is the

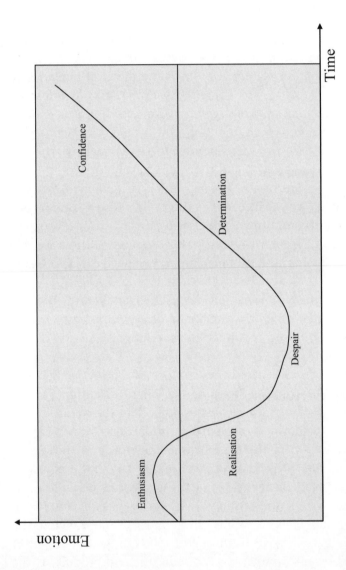

Figure 7.3   Emotional journey – supporters

main source of the requirement for positive emotional energy. Moreover, it is not coincidental that the emotional journey for the wider community tends to follow a similar pattern, as illustrated in Figure 7.4.

After initial curiosity, natural conservatism usually takes over as stakeholders identify real or perceived threats to their interests, and anxiety over those concerns deepens into resistance when shared with others and confronted with the real prospect of change. It is an absolute priority for the business case author in the early stages of the work to surface that resistance and not to fear it or to try to tiptoe around the areas of vulnerability. As in all change processes, the resistance will come out sooner or later, and dealing with it early and openly is much the best option. By surfacing the resistance, working to address each specific concern as far as possible and following the communications strategy, the team can earn the respect of the wider stakeholder community and, with a bit of luck and strong sponsorship, secure their ultimate acceptance of the business case.

Leading everyone on this journey will secure the different outcomes required at each stage of the work. At first the focus will be on winning buy-in to the objectives of the project and to the business case process itself. Later, as the analysis firms up, the focus will shift to selling the preferred option. Finally, once it looks as if the recommended decision is assured, the focus can move on to mobilising support for implementation.

At every stage, it is trust which is the key. Any good book on selling will emphasise the critical importance of trust to

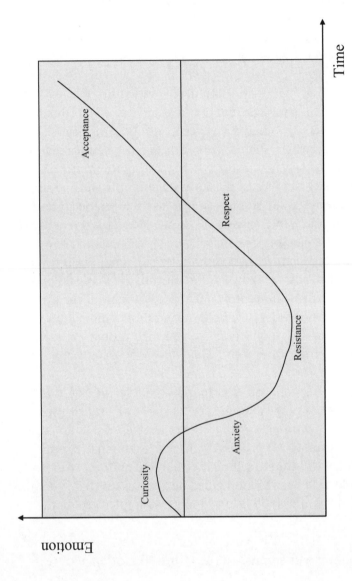

Figure 7.4   Emotional journey – wider community

winning a sale. Winning the argument on the business case is similar. People are more likely to be persuaded by someone who knows what they are talking about and in whose intentions and abilities they have confidence. This leads right back to the discussion in Chapter 1 about what makes a good business case, and the goal of producing business cases characterised both by competence and by integrity. Do the work thoroughly, systematically and professionally, and decision makers will be persuaded by your competence and expertise. Demonstrate integrity and show the positive energy and commitment to get behind your team and your task, and decision makers will want to be persuaded. In this way, the hard work to make the case will be backed up as it deserves to be by the equally hard work to win the argument.

Conclusion

This chapter has explained how to win the argument for the business case through effective stakeholder management and communications. It is vital to appreciate that stakeholder management and communications must run from the very beginning to the very end of your work. Specific instances where engagement with stakeholders is imperative have been mentioned throughout the book and this chapter summarises the approach rather than trying to capture them all. Stakeholder management is pervasive and cannot be confined to one workstream in a business case team any more than to one chapter in a book.

There are three components to the overall approach recommended here:

1. *Stakeholder mapping.* Start by identifying the stakeholders in the project and map them on to a two-by-two matrix according to their relative power and their relative stake in the project.

2. *Communications.* Each of the four groups on the stakeholder map requires a distinct communications approach. Use existing one-way channels to get your message to those with least power and stake in the project, and make sure you focus on aspects of greatest concern to them. Consult those who have a significant stake but little power – but be realistic and honest about the scope of the consultation. Tailor communications individually to stakeholders with power, listening carefully to their concerns and responding to them, holding one-to-one meetings wherever possible and ensuring that those with a significant stake in the project are kept fully informed. Do not neglect internal communications – your team need to know what is going on and to develop protocols for working together effectively.

3. *Leadership.* As the business case author, it is your role to lead both the team and wider stakeholder community on the emotional journey of the business case, working through the inevitable crises of confidence and stakeholder resistance to earn trust in your competence and integrity and eventual acceptance of the business case.

WINNING THE ARGUMENT (7)

Chapter 7 Exercise: The Amazon Project

The Amazon Project, a mid-sized charitable organisation whose goals are to preserve the Brazilian rainforest and support sustainable development for its inhabitants, has received a conditional offer of a very large donation from Mr Julius, a wealthy celebrity who wishes to purchase and preserve a substantial tract of rainforest. The Board has asked you to prepare a business case. In the task definition stage, you have established that the budget is a fixed, but generous, amount and that the Board is really looking for a recommendation as to whether they should accept the donation at all and, if they should, what the shape of the project should be; they are not at this stage looking for a choice of site or a detailed implementation plan.

Marcus, one of the non-executive directors, has written the Chief Executive a pompous and, in the CE's view, ill-informed letter about the imperative of protecting the Amazon Project's charitable status and raising the alarm about its exposure to foreign taxes. Crassus, the other non-executive director, is worried that the proposal will absorb all the energies of the organisation, shifting attention away from its more community-based work. Claudia, the long-serving and vocal Outreach Director, feels the approach is colonialist and contradicts the organisation's partnership-based mission. The other three executive directors are keeping their counsel, perhaps waiting to see which way the wind blows.

The small staff of 30 do not know about the offer but have heard rumours of a major change of focus and are anxious about their existing projects. Cleo, the charity's communications assistant who has been drafted into your business case team, approached you yesterday to ask what she could say in next week's partnership meeting with the anti-logging activist group GreenTrees.

Your sponsor, the Chief Executive, believes this is a huge opportunity for the organisation, but accepts that it must be done right if it is to work and if he is to carry the Board with him. He believes the key to achieving a consensus lies in a proper understanding of the range of stakeholders who need to be persuaded of the merits of the proposal. Draw a stakeholder map, showing the individuals and groups you think need to be considered, and list the five or six top priority actions in your stakeholder management strategy.

(8) Completing a Successful Business Case

The last stages in the business case endeavour are as important as all the others, and it can be a challenge to hang on to the energy, commitment, rigour and resources needed to finish the job to the highest standards. While there is no particular methodology to apply to what is often a diffuse and protracted stage in the proceedings, there are generally four milestones to attain – completion, presentation, decision and handover/closure.

Completion

Once the options appraisal is done, completing the business case may be a matter of tying up loose ends of data and polishing the text and diagrams, if there is time for that, or it may be a more substantial piece of work for which you should allow time in the plan. It depends on the ground the organisation requires the business case to cover.

It is often necessary to say something about sources of funds. Is the money available to meet the investment cost? What is the net cash position in each financial year and how will any shortfalls be managed? If the preferred option involves a partnership or joint venture of any kind, who is putting up the money and what is the basis of sharing costs and benefits?

Sometimes it is expected that the business case will incorporate specific procurement advice, setting out the procurement approach for the preferred option or even, in some circumstances, recommending the choice of one supplier over another and providing a detailed justification. Other common additional expectations – particularly but not exclusively in the public sector – are impact assessments, analysing the impact of the proposals on, for example, workforce diversity, the environment, or regulatory burdens.

Try to negotiate a common sense approach to completion. Document length often becomes an issue at this stage, and there is little room for material which is surplus to the requirements for a decision. Nevertheless, compliance is an important objective, and it is better to have more annexes than you might really want than to court negative judgements by falling short of expectations and requirements.

Presentation

Unless the decision-making process is completely closed, such as for example in the case of some grant applications, there is sure to be at least one opportunity to talk to decision makers, individually or collectively or preferably both, about the decision they are to make.

This is the moment for the presenter – whether sponsor, author, business case team, or all three – to be passionate about the project and the preferred option. Do not offer the audience a dull recitation of an arid slide pack rehearsing the detail from each section of the document. Be a vigorous advocate instead, confident that your advocacy will be respected because you have done the work with competence and integrity and there is nothing to hide. In the most common case where a decision is made by a board of some kind, these considerations hold as true for the essential pre-positioning meetings as they do for the board meeting itself. Every decision maker needs to be convinced:

- that the project objectives are the right ones, and fit the wider strategy;

- that the preferred option is the best choice;

- that it is going to work;

- that their concerns have been met; and

- that the team has done a professional job which they can trust.

Practise the presentation beforehand. At a minimum do a full run-through with the team, and if possible arrange a 'red team' review, recruiting one or two friendly neutrals to critique the presentation and ask awkward questions.

Decision

If the decision is made to accept the recommendation in the business case, celebrate your success with your team and go on to handover/closure as quickly as possible.

It is also important, however, for you as business case author to be psychologically prepared to handle a negative decision and to be able to minimise the damage to the organisation, to the team and to yourself. Anyone who has ever worked on a project which has been cancelled, come second in a bidding process, or lost out in a job interview (which is surely most of us), knows that there is little consolation to be had in being thanked for your efforts. Nevertheless the priority must be to enable organisation and individuals alike to move on and make best use of the experience and knowledge they have gained through the business case development process.

Regardless of whether the project is stopped altogether, or a non-recommended option selected, the analytical work done in the business case, particularly on strategic objectives and on identification of costs, benefits and risks, will have influenced future thinking, and represents a mine of information which should be of great value to those developing a new approach to the issues. Orderly closure is therefore of just as much importance in these circumstances. Individuals, too, will have learned and if they have done good work their reputations should be enhanced by it. It is the role of the team leader to coach team members to show mature acceptance of an adverse decision and move on. The same applies to the business case author, who has no doubt worked hardest of all and had to show the deepest commitment. Remember this is a project, not a cause, and those who took the decision were entitled to take it; there is neither virtue nor reward in sabotage or sulking.

Handover/Closure

The work of the business case team is done either way. If the decision is made to proceed with the preferred option, the top priority will be mobilisation. Mobilisation obviously means resourcing and recruiting a project team and putting project management processes in place, but that is a separate responsibility. From the perspective of handing over the business case, mobilisation (see Figure 1.1) is about mobilising support for the project, providing a platform for managing it and providing a baseline for measuring it.

Mobilising support involves working with the new project manager and project owner to give them a full understanding of the stakeholder management work which has been carried out in the course of developing the business case. The communications strategy pursued during the business case stage will need to be developed for the implementation stage, preferably using the same media (where they have proved effective). Stakeholders who have been consulted will expect their input to be at least acknowledged by the project team and preferably demonstrably incorporated into the implementation plan. Resistance from those who are or perceive themselves to be at risk of being adversely affected by the chosen option can be expected to enjoy a new lease of life following the decision, even if the business case team has successfully damped it down, and the project team needs to understand in detail the line of argument which has been used with these stakeholders and any concessions which have been made.

The business case will provide a platform for managing the project if the project manager understands and values it, and feels able to put his or her own stamp on project organisation without having to start again from scratch. The key elements of the business case in this respect are the implementation plan, the risk register, the benefits map and the cost model. These need to be explained in depth to the incoming project manager, who will no doubt wish to challenge, amplify and elaborate all of them, beginning the necessary process of digging down to another level of detail. Nothing should be assumed. It is not unknown for project managers to regard, or even be encouraged to regard, the business case as a vehicle for securing funding which has now done its job and does not even merit reading. This is a terrible waste.

Finally, the business case should be used by the organisation as a baseline for measuring the performance of the project. Control over performance metrics is often a sensitive issue, particularly if they are linked to remuneration, and exactly how measurement is carried out is an argument in which you do not need to get involved. It is not necessarily either the project manager's fault or the business case author's fault if certain costs turn out to be higher than anticipated – change is to be expected. What is important is to recognise that the business case was the basis on which the decision was made, and sooner or later the organisation should, and may well be required to, evaluate that decision by looking at whether the implementation is delivering the benefits envisaged at the budgeted cost to the planned timetable. Planning for that evaluation means that the final business case must be clearly identified as such, using robust version labelling and document protection to prevent subsequent 'tweaking', and stored in both the paper and electronic record.

Conclusion

This book has explained how to produce an outstanding business case. At the beginning, I defined a business case as a recommendation to decision makers to take a particular course of action for the organisation, supported by an analysis of its benefits, costs and risks compared to the realistic alternatives, with an explanation of how it can best be implemented. The standard of business cases produced in both the public and private sectors is highly variable, and delivering a strong case calls on you to demonstrate both integrity and competence. Competence does not require any deep technical skill and can be greatly enhanced by following the practical steps set out in this book.

The key steps are:

- defining the task clearly from the outset (Chapter 2);

- developing a strong case for change and a shortlist of viable options (Chapter 3);

- identifying and quantifying the benefits of the project and assessing how well each option will deliver them (Chapter 4);

- building a financial model to capture the costs, savings and revenues each option will produce (Chapter 5);

- assessing the risks associated with the options, planning their implementation timetables and weighing the options against each other (Chapter 6);

- communicating with your stakeholders throughout the work on the business case and earning their trust (Chapter 7).

Following this approach should enable you to do a professional job, and to make a real contribution to good decision making and the private and public good which flows from it.

(9) Model Answers to the Exercises

Chapter 2 Exercise: Young Brothers

You will have phrased your questions in your own way, of course, but you should have covered the same sort of ground as the following, and struck a comparably direct tone. You risk letting your client down, and damaging your local reputation, if you do not get the boundaries of the task clear up front.

1. Who is the business case for? Are you the decision maker, or do you need the approval of your Board, or of a financial institution or an investment partner?

2. What decisions have already been taken? Is this just one possible growth strategy or are you already committed to internet marketing and direct distribution?

3. What sort of options do you want to compare? Are you interested primarily in the business and financial evidence for a go/no-go decision, or in evaluating implementation options (e.g. a joint venture with an external marketing partner) or both?

4. Have you decided how much you are prepared to invest in this? What are your borrowing limits?

5. What sort of final output are you looking for? Is a formal document of value, or do you just want answers?

Chapter 3 Exercise: Irish Wind Farms

There would be a lot of hard work to do to gather the detailed evidence which a business case for a major political and investment decision of this kind would need, and crafting a preferred option which could command a political consensus would be very challenging. But a good answer here will show powerfully how relatively easy it is to bring a clarity of structure to the process.

a) Your list of strategies should be long, and you may well have thought of some not included here. Among the more important:

-   National energy strategy.

-   EU carbon emissions strategy and targets and Government of Ireland implementation plan.

-   Public-private partnership strategy.

-   National and regional employment strategies.

-   West of Ireland tourism strategy.

-   Regional community development strategies.

-   Irish language strategy.

- Major energy companies' wind power strategies.

- Other countries' alternative energy strategies (for benchmarking).

b) Tabulating the drivers will help with preparing a strong case for change, which is certain to be needed. Your table should look something like Table 9.1.

c) A wide range of options can be imagined at this early stage. Noting that the zero option has been ruled out, but that there are some treacherous political and economic waters to navigate, it would be a good idea to keep a fairly broad spread of options available. You might, for example, have thought about:

- *One mega-farm.* This could minimise the number of communities adversely affected, create an industrial

Table 9.1   Chapter 3 exercise: drivers for Irish wind farms project

Driver	Description	Category	Strength	Ownership	Evidence
Energy security	Need to supply x per cent of own energy needs	Energy	Critical – aspect of national security	Energy Minister	Energy Strategy
Carbon emissions	Need to cut emissions by x per cent by 20YY	Environment	Critical – EU obligation and political imperative	Taoiseach	EU directive. Speeches/ published policies
Local economy	Stop or slow depopulation in rural/Irish language areas	Communities	Important but contested – focus on long-term jobs	Employment Minister/ Regional authorities	Regional economic data

landmark in its own right, and might have economies of scale from the private sector partner's point of view.

- *A network of micro-farms.* This could limit local environmental impact and enhance local sustainability, spread the employment benefits, and make it practical to work with several private sector partners.

- *Decentralisation.* Government could introduce incentives and/or penalties to encourage providers to source a rising percentage of their supply from wind turbines, and establish a national licensing framework within which local authorities and companies could negotiate their own projects in the interests of their electorates and shareholders.

Chapter 4 Exercise: Eastport Pier

This is quite a challenging exercise, but offers some very important lessons. The first of these is that benefits mapping is a collective exercise which has an important function in developing consensus and flushing out differences. I have no doubt that your benefits map will look different from mine and from that of every other person who does this exercise individually. The map presented in Figure 9.1 has no more validity than any other and while that drawn by an experienced local authority officer in a seaside town would undoubtedly contain deeper insights than mine or yours, it would not be in any meaningful sense 'right' either. Only through collective effort is it possible to use the benefits map to tease out all

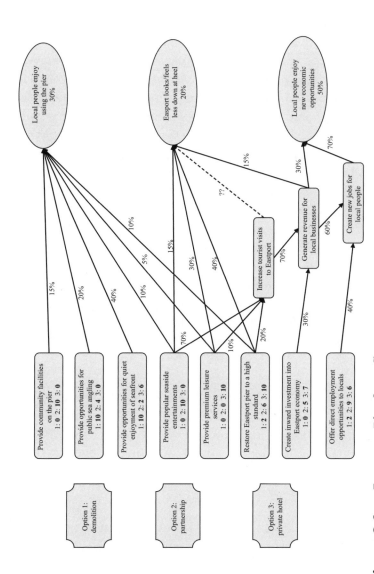

Figure 9.1   Eastport Pier benefits map

the issues and produce something commanding a measure of consensus.

Figure 9.1 is somewhat more complex than the example given in the chapter itself, because a secondary output layer has been introduced. The presentational difficulty this creates is easy to see, but it seemed unavoidable here in order not to oversimplify economic effects to a degree which would distort the outcome. Unlike the Irish wind farms example in the chapter, the analysis in the accompanying tables shows one option having a very clear lead over the other two as far as benefits are concerned.

Remember that this does not make it the preferred option. This is partly because no consideration has yet been given to cost or achievability. You should not have factored into your benefits map the fact that the private hotel developer was prepared to pay more, both upfront and in business rates, than the Option 2 consortium, because these are monetary amounts and will be captured in the cost analysis.

By far the most important lesson from this exercise, however, is the imperative of using the benefits mapping, weighting and scoring process to tackle issues of substance. The quantitative methodology is worthless if the issues of substance it throws up are not thoroughly addressed. In this case, there are at least four:

1. *Tourism strategy.* Is there one? The map in Figure 9.1 presumes that increased tourism will not improve the image of Eastport, about which locals expressed such concern in the survey.

Table 9.2 Chapter 4 exercise (Eastport Pier) benefits map calculations: weighting

		Weighting	Contribution	Weighted value
Output 1	Provide community facilities on the pier			
	Local people enjoy using the pier	30%	15%	4.5%
	Total weighted value			4.5%
Output 2	Provide opportunities for public sea angling			
	Local people enjoy using the pier	30%	20%	6.0%
	Total weighted value			6.0%
Output 3	Provide opportunities for quiet enjoyment of the seafront			
	Local people enjoy using the pier	30%	40%	12.0%
	Total weighted value			12.0%
Output 4	Provide popular seaside entertainments			
	Local people enjoy using the pier	30%	10%	3.0%
	Eastport looks/feels less down at heel			
	– Direct route	20%	15%	3.0%
	– Route via increased tourism and revenue for local businesses	20%	7.4%	1.5%
	Local people enjoy new economic opportunities			
	– Route via increased tourism and revenue for local businesses	50%	14.7%	7.4%
	– Route via increased tourism, revenue for local businesses, and new jobs	50%	20.6%	10.3%
	Total weighted value			25.1%
Output 5	Provide premium leisure services			
	Local people enjoy using the pier	30%	5%	1.5%
	Eastport looks/feels less down at heel			
	– Direct route	20%	30%	6.0%
	– Route via increased tourism and revenue for local businesses	20%	1.1%	0.2%
	Local people enjoy new economic opportunities			
	– Route via increased tourism and revenue for local businesses	50%	2.1%	1.1%
	– Route via increased tourism, revenue for local businesses, and new jobs	50%	2.9%	1.5%
	Total weighted value			10.2%
Output 6	Restore Eastport pier to a high standard			
	Local people enjoy using the pier	30%	10%	3.0%
	Eastport looks/feels less down at heel			
	– Direct route	20%	40%	8.0%
	– Route via increased tourism and revenue for local businesses	20%	2.1%	0.4%
	Local people enjoy new economic opportunities			
	– Route via increased tourism and revenue for local businesses	50%	4.2%	2.1%
	– Route via increased tourism, revenue for local businesses, and new jobs	50%	5.9%	2.9%
	Total weighted value			16.5%
Output 7	Create inward investment into Eastport economy			
	Eastport looks/feels less down at heel			
	– Route via revenue for local businesses	20%	4.5%	0.9%
	Local people enjoy new economic opportunities			
	– Route via revenue for local businesses	50%	9.0%	4.5%
	– Route via revenue for local businesses, and new jobs	50%	12.6%	6.3%
	Total weighted value			11.7%
Output 8	Offer direct employment opportunities to locals			
	Local people enjoy new economic opportunities			
	– Route via new jobs	50%	28.0%	14.0%
	Total weighted value			14.0%
Check	Sum of total weighted values should be 100%			100.0%

This is a fundamental strategic choice for the local authority – do they want a quiet retirement town or a bustling resort? Or do they think they can have both? How?

2. *Social impact of Option 2*. Will putting an amusement arcade and a nightclub on the pier create a thriving social centre,

Table 9.3   Chapter 4 exercise (Eastport Pier) benefits map calculations: scoring

Option		Outputs								Total	Rank
		1	*2*	*3*	*4*	*5*	*6*	*7*	*8*		
	Weighted Value	*4.5*	*6*	*12*	*25.1*	*10.2*	*16.5*	*11.7*	*14*		
Option 1	Score	0	10	10	0	0	2	0	2		
	Weighted score	0	60	120	0	0	33	0	28	**241**	**3**
Option 2	Score	10	4	2	10	0	6	5	9		
	Weighted score	45	24	24	251	0	99	59	126	**627**	**1**
Option 3	Score	0	0	6	0	10	10	7	6		
	Weighted score	0	0	72	0	102	165	82	84	**505**	**2**

resolving some of the current youth alienation problems, or will it become a focus for antisocial behaviour? There are major benefits and/or disbenefits at stake here, and some thorough research into the experience of other seaside towns is essential.

3. *Value of special interests.* The quantitative challenge of how to weight the interests of the sea anglers, who are few in number but feel very strongly about their hobby, goes right to the heart of ancient political debates both inside and outside utilitarianism and will no doubt have contemporary political resonance for local councillors who know that people express their feelings at the ballot box. There is no right answer, but focusing on benefits empowers the business case author to bring the question on to the table and insist that it be openly addressed.

4. *Econometric modelling.* Whether a single substantial inward investment from Dubai would generate more prosperity for local people by stimulating economic activity in the local supply chain than would the opportunity for local small businesses to operate concessions on the pier is not just a matter of opinion; an evidence-based econometric model needs to be written to model the impact of different scenarios over time. This requires expert input, which in turn requires both time and money in the production of the business case.

Chapter 5 Exercise: Truly Enormous Bank

Do not be too harsh on Luster – he has not done a bad job. But there are some causes for anxiety. Your email might be along the following lines:

'The presentation is clear, there are no obvious omissions from the cost and revenue lines, and the assumptions are well documented and to a large extent appear to be based on an appropriate level of research. The project may be worth doing. I do have three areas of concern, however.

First, and most fundamentally, the treatment of the receipt from the sale of the freehold premises in Ashby is incorrect. Selling this asset diminishes the bank's fixed assets, and while TEB is not a property investment company and this may be a perfectly rational decision, it is a separate decision from the opening of an office in Swadlincote. The £180K receipt could no doubt be realised through a sale and leaseback arrangement if we so wished, without moving the branch six miles down the road. The appraisal should be redone, excluding this figure and, as a corollary, including the residual value of the Swadlincote lease premium after 5 years and any rental income which we know we could obtain for the vacated premises as Ashby. This would reduce a strongly positive NPV at 8 per cent right down to the margin, which is where I believe the decision truly lies.

Second, I would like to see some sensitivity analysis on the revenue figures. This of course assumes much greater importance if the decision is seen as more marginal than currently presented. How confident is Luster that there will be a net growth of 500 in branch accounts? Is he not expecting to lose a number of accounts from Ashby residents when that branch closes? Has he considered any possible offsetting negative impact on the Burton branch from customers in the villages between Swadlincote and Burton switching accounts to the new branch? With how much confidence can we really expect to add and retain a further 500 accounts in year 2 with only a limited local advertising campaign?

Third, the costing of additional staff seems too casual. They are based solely on salaries, and take no account of employer's national insurance and pension contributions. No provision is made for the costs of recruiting and training new staff, or for incentives or allowances to support the apparent assumption that all existing Ashby staff will simply relocate. Year on year revenue growth is assumed, but no provision is made for pay rises over the same period.'

Chapter 6 Exercise: Power Station in Space

For a daring option such as this, your risk register could be very long indeed! The important things about this exercise are to get you used to using the risk register format and to emphasise the paramount importance of intelligent commentary and analysis in highlighting for decision makers the sometimes quite subtle strategic and tactical implications of their decision. The risk register can never be added up, but properly used it can take people deeper down to another level of reflection.

Table 9.4   Risk Register for Chapter 6 exercise: power station in space

No.	Risk title	Description	Impact	Probability	Rating	Commentary/ Mitigation
1	Development failure	The five-year laboratory development phase may identify technical problems which take significant additional cost and time to overcome.	8	7	15 (Red)	Impact mitigated by already generous development timetable including contingency for problem resolution. Probability is hard to assess; could be reduced if open access to US/Russian lessons learned can be negotiated.
2	Damage during construction	Sensitive components cannot be fully protected against orbiting debris in the construction phase and are exposed to damage.	6	6	12 (Amber)	Statistical modelling underpins the probability score. Impact would depend on components affected; worst result would be additional shuttle missions, adding time and cost.
3	Partnership failure	Ireland would be only a minor partner in the project. Withdrawal or demands for change from major partners could cause serious disruption or even cancellation.	9	9	18 (Purple)	Opposition in Poland, ahead in opinion polls, has said it would pull out. Italian negotiators are already causing delays over workshare arrangements. A commercial protection strategy and a milestone-based exit strategy of our own are essential.

Table 9.4   *Concluded*

4	Relative price movements	Energy storage and transmission costs will be high, and a small decline in oil prices could choke off demand for space-sourced energy even at marginal cost.	9	5	14 (Red)	Little can be done to mitigate impact, which would turn the project into a mistimed white elephant. Few serious commentators predict a long-term decline in oil prices, however, and the economic model is robust against short-term fluctuations in demand.
5	Delivery vehicle catastrophe	Suspension of shuttle services following a catastrophic incident such as befell Challenger and Discovery would halt contruction.	5	3	8 (Green)	Independent assessments of NASA's safety procedures show major improvements. In the event of suspension, service could be negotiated from Russia, though not without time and cost implications.

Your risk register might not look very like the model answer in Table 9.4 above and you may have stressed quite different key points, but you should at least have drawn attention to risks covering an unusually wide range, and made the point strongly in your commentary that this was not a safe option and an active approach to mitigation would be essential. A commentary to accompany the model register might run as follows:

'This is a high-risk option, as you would expect from any venture at the technological frontier. The most serious risk is political. We have only limited muscle at the negotiating table and cannot eliminate the vulnerability of the project to problems in the multilateral partnership. Securing a robust commercial agreement, with stiff penalties to bind in successor administrations, is absolutely essential if the risk associated this option is to be considered acceptable. Moreover, it will be important to ensure that our financial commitments are limited in the early stages, and fallback plans kept in place, to enable a low-cost exit in the event of insuperable issues of either a political or a technical nature in the development phase. While the construction and safety risks are considerable, they do not make the option unachievable and need to be considered alongside the environmental risks of other options. The exposure to market fluctuations in the price of more conventional energy sources is not a disproportionate risk for a long-term capital project such as this. In summary, there is a real risk that this option may fail, and it should not be entered into, whatever its attractions, without a robust fallback plan and an honest presentation of the risks to stakeholders and taxpayers.'

Chapter 7 Exercise: The Amazon Project

The stakeholder map is relatively simple; anything along the general lines of Figure 9.2 will be more than adequate. The difficulty is planning what is sure to be an exceptionally delicate communications campaign.

This proposal could collapse within days if an effective stakeholder management strategy is not implemented right

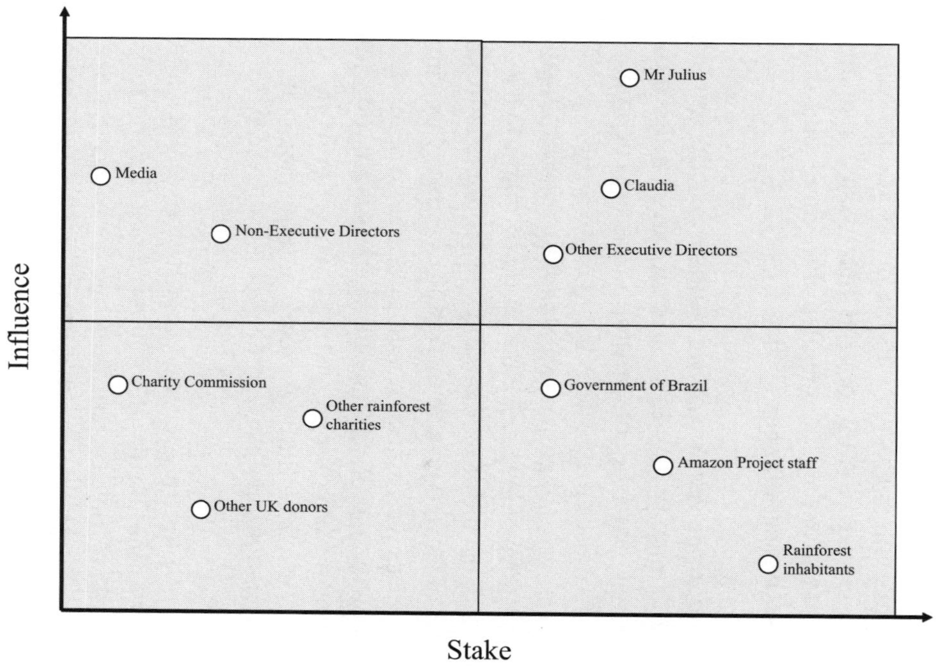

Figure 9.2   Amazon Project stakeholder map

away. Your list of top priority actions should demonstrate a differentiated approach to the range of stakeholders and a sense of urgency. It might include:

- Individual interviews with all the directors, and with Mr Julius; you need to flush out the interests and opinions of those who have not yet revealed their hand, and start to explore the space for consensus.

- An options development workshop with the executive directors only; you and your sponsor need to draw them into some ownership of the proposal, or it is doomed.

- A field survey, supported by some desk research, to assess the attitudes of local people who do or might live within a protected rainforest area, and the economic and social impact of foreign private ownership.

- Work with a professional media consultant (Mr Julius probably already has one on retainer) to frame the story for the celebrity-hungry media and manage the leaks which look inevitable.

- An all-staff meeting for the Chief Executive to give them some information about what you are doing and reassure them about their current projects. Try to agree a neutral line with all the executive directors so that they get used to standing together.

- Formal meetings with relevant authorities who may be in a position to disrupt the proposal, particularly the Government of Brazil and perhaps also the Charity Commission and the tax authorities.

- A separate mapping exercise to identify those NGOs (non-governmental organisations) who might be expected to see either a threat or an opportunity in the proposal. In the light of this work, line up the Chief Executive to brief some of his counterparts over a few lunches and coffees.

If you have found this resource useful you may be interested in other titles from Gower

59 Checklists for Project and Programme Management
Second Edition
Rudy Kor and Gert Wijnen
Paperback: 224 pages; 244 x 172 mm
978-0-566-08775-2; eISBN: 978-0-7546-8191-5

Communicating Strategy
Phil Jones
Paperback: 198 pages; 244 x 172 mm
978-0-566-08810-0; eISBN: 978-0-7546-8288-2

Critical Chain
Eli Goldratt
Paperback: 254 pages; 234 x 156 mm
978-0-566-08038-8

Essentials of Project Management
Third Edition
Dennis Lock
Paperback: 218 pages; 244 x 172 mm
978-0-566-08805-6

The Goal
A Process of Ongoing Improvement
Third Edition
Eliyahu M. Goldratt and Jeff Cox
Paperback: 400 pages; 229 x 153 mm
978-0-566-08665-6

Project Leadership
Second Edition
Wendy Briner, Colin Hastings and Michael Geddes
Paperback: 176 pages; 234 x 156 mm
978-0-566-07785-2

Benefit Realisation Management
A Practical Guide to Achieving Benefits Through Change
Gerald Bradley
Hardback: 312 pages; 244 x 172 mm
978-0-566-08687-8

GOWER

Gower Handbook of Programme Management
Geoff Reiss, Malcolm Anthony, John Chapman, Geof Leigh, Adrian
Pyne and Paul Rayner
Hardback: 738 pages; 244 x 172 mm
978-0-566-08603-8

Gower Handbook of Project Management
Fourth Edition
Edited by Rodney Turner
Hardback: 912 pages; 244 x 172 mm
978-0-566-08806-3

Project Reviews, Assurance and Governance
Graham Oakes
Hardback: 288 pages; 244 x 172 mm
978-0-566-08807-0; eISBN: 978-0-7546-8146-5

Using Earned Value
Alan Webb
Hardback: 152 pages; 244 x 172 mm
978-0-566-08533-8

Go to:
www.gowerpublishing.com/projectmanagement
for details of these and our wide range of project
management titles.

Visit **www.gowerpublishing.com** and

- search the entire catalogue of Gower books in print
- order titles online at 10% discount
- take advantage of special offers
- sign up for our monthly e-mail update service
- download free sample chapters from all recent titles
- download or order our catalogue